THE
DANGERS
OF PRE-TRIBULATIONISM

THE
DANGERS
OF PRE-TRIBULATIONISM

A Supplementary Analysis
to When Will the Messiah Return?

J.K. McKee

TNN PRESS
www.tnnonline.net

The Dangers
of Pre-Tribulationism

Cover photos: Istockphoto

Published by TNN Press, a division of Outreach Israel Ministries
908 Audelia Rd. Suite 200-228
Richardson, Texas 75081
(407) 933-2002

www.tnnonline.net/tnnpress

Unless otherwise noted, Scripture quotations are from the *New American Standard, Updated Edition* (NASU), © 1995, The Lockman Foundation.

TABLE OF CONTENTS

ABBREVIATION CHART AND SPECIAL TERMS

The following is a chart of abbreviations for reference works and special terms that are used in publications by TNN Press. Please familiarize yourself with them as the text may reference a Bible version, i.e., RSV for the Revised Standard Version, or a source such as TWOT for the Theological Wordbook of the Old Testament, solely by its abbreviation. Detailed listings of these sources are provided in the Bibliography.

Special terms that may be used have been provided in this chart:

ABD: *Anchor Bible Dictionary*

AMG: *Complete Word Study Dictionary: Old Testament, New Testament*

ANE: Ancient Near East(ern)

Apostolic Scriptures/Writings: the New Testament

Ara: Aramaic

ATS: ArtScroll Tanach (1996)

b. Babylonian Talmud (*Talmud Bavli*)

B.C.E.: Before Common Era or B.C.

BDAG: *A Greek-English Lexicon of the New Testament and Other Early Christian Literature* (Bauer, Danker, Arndt, Gingrich)

BDB: *Brown-Driver-Briggs Hebrew and English Lexicon*

BECNT: *Baker Exegetical Commentary on the New Testament*

BKCNT: *Bible Knowledge Commentary: New Testament*

C.E.: Common Era or A.D.

CEV: Contemporary English Version (1995)

CGEDNT: *Concise Greek-English Dictionary of New Testament Words* (Barclay M. Newman)

CHALOT: *Concise Hebrew and Aramaic Lexicon of the Old Testament*

CJB: Complete Jewish Bible (1998)

DRA: *Douay-Rheims American Edition*

DSS: Dead Sea Scrolls

ECB: *Eerdmans Commentary on the Bible*

EDB: *Eerdmans Dictionary of the Bible*

eisegesis: "reading meaning into," or interjecting a preconceived or foreign meaning into a Biblical text

EJ: *Encylopaedia Judaica*

ESV: English Standard Version (2001)

exegesis: "drawing meaning out of," or the process of trying to understand what a Biblical text means on its own

EXP: *Expositor's Bible Commentary*

Ger: German

GNT: Greek New Testament

Grk: Greek

halachah: lit. "the way to walk," how the Torah is lived out in an individual's life or faith community

HALOT: *Hebrew & Aramaic Lexicon of the Old Testament* (Koehler and Baumgartner)

HCSB: Holman Christian Standard Bible (2004)

Heb: Hebrew

HNV: Hebrew Names Version of the World English Bible

ICC: *International Critical Commentary*

IDB: *Interpreter's Dictionary of the Bible*

IDBSup: *Interpreter's Dictionary of the Bible Supplement*

ISBE: *International Standard Bible Encyclopedia*

IVPBBC: *IVP Bible Background Commentary (Old & New Testament)*

Jastrow. *Dictionary of the Targumim, Talmud Bavli, Talmud Yerushalmi, and Midrashic Literature* (Marcus Jastrow)

JBK: New Jerusalem Bible-Koren (2000)

JETS: *Journal of the Evangelical Theological Society*

KJV: King James Version

Lattimore: The New Testament by Richmond Lattimore (1996)

LITV: *Literal Translation of the Holy Bible* by Jay P. Green (1986)

LS: *A Greek-English Lexicon* (Liddell & Scott)

LXE: *Septuagint with Apocrypha* by Sir L.C.L. Brenton (1851)

LXX: Septuagint

m. Mishnah

MT: Masoretic Text

NASB: New American Standard Bible (1977)

NASU: New American Standard Update (1995)

NBCR: *New Bible Commentary: Revised*

NEB: New English Bible (1970)

Nelson: *Nelson's Expository Dictionary of Old Testament Words*

NETS: New English Translation of the Septuagint (2007)

NIB: *New Interpreter's Bible*

NIGTC: *New International Greek Testament Commentary*

NICNT: *New International Commentary on the New Testament*

NIDB: *New International Dictionary of the Bible*

NIV: New International Version (1984)

NJB: New Jerusalem Bible-Catholic (1985)

NJPS: Tanakh, A New Translation of the Holy Scriptures (1999)

NKJV: New King James Version (1982)

NRSV: New Revised Standard Version (1989)

NLT: New Living Translation (1996)

NT: New Testament

orthopraxy:- lit. "the right action," how the Bible or one's theology is lived out in the world

OT: Old Testament

PreachC: *The Preacher's Commentary*

REB: Revised English Bible (1989)

RSV: Revised Standard Version (1952)

t. Tosefta

Tanach (Tanakh): the Old Testament

Thayer: *Thayer's Greek-English Lexicon of the New Testament*

TDNT: *Theological Dictionary of the New Testament*

TEV: Today's English Version (1976)

TLV: Tree of Life Messianic Family Bible—New Covenant (2011)

TNIV: Today's New International Version (2005)

TNTC: *Tyndale New Testament Commentaries*

TWOT: *Theological Wordbook of the Old Testament*

UBSHNT: United Bible Societies' 1991 Hebrew New Testament revised edition

v(s). verse(s)

Vine: *Vine's Complete Expository Dictionary of Old and New Testament Words*

Vul: Latin Vulgate

WBC: *Word Biblical Commentary*

Yid: Yiddish

YLT: Young's Literal Translation (1862/1898)

Forward
Is the Doctrine of Pre-Tribulation Rapture Valid or Invalid?

by Jane J. McKee

"The end is near!" is a popular phrase heard around the world today. Many believe that Messiah is coming any day—possibly today—to take us to heaven before the Tribulation. Whether or not there will be a Pre-Tribulation or a Post-Tribulation rapture is one of the most controversial subjects today. I believe there will be a Post-Tribulation rapture because Jesus says it, Paul reiterates it, and John the Beloved explains it.

The doctrine of Pre-Tribulation rapture is preached in pulpits across the world as a known fact when in truth Jesus Himself says the exact opposite. In Matthew 24:29-31, He says, "Immediately after the tribulation of those days shall the sun be darkened, and the moon shall not give her light, and the stars shall fall from heaven, and the powers of the heavens shall be shaken (see Revelation 6:12-13): And then shall appear the sign of the son of man in heaven: and then shall all the tribes of the earth mourn, and they shall see the son of man coming in the clouds of heaven with power and great glory. And he shall send his angels with a great sound of a trumpet, and they shall gather together his elect from the four winds, from one end of heaven to the other." In saying this, Jesus clearly states that Believers will go through the Tribulation.

Another commonly misinterpreted passage is 1 Thessalonians 4:16-18. In this Paul says, "For the Lord himself shall descend from heaven with a shout, with the voice of the archangel, and with the trump of God: and the dead in Messiah shall rise first: Then we which are alive and remain shall be caught up with them in the clouds, to meet the Lord in the air: and so shall we ever be with the Lord. Wherefore comfort one another with these words." In saying those that are alive and remain, Paul is inferring to the ones who survive the Tribulation who are also called the assembly of Philadelphia in Revelation. Earlier in 1 Thessalonians 3:13, Paul said that Jesus would come back with his Tribulation saints, which in logical thinking would infer that the Tribulation had already happened. These Tribulation saints are known as the "non-survivors" or the assembly of Smyrna in Revelation. Also, in 1 Corinthians 15:52, Paul says, "In a moment, in the twinkling of an eye, at the LAST TRUMP: for the trumpet shall sound, and the dead shall be raised incorruptible, and we shall be changed." This is a more specific verse of the time of the rapture than 1 Thessalonians 4:16-18 but it says basically the same thing.

John the Beloved says in Revelation 11:15-17, "And the seventh angel sounded; and there were great voices in heaven, saying, The kingdoms of this world are become the kingdoms of our Lord, and of his Messiah; and he shall reign for ever and ever. And the four and twenty elders, which sat before God on their seats, fell upon their faces, and worshipped God, Saying, We give thee thanks, O Lord God Almighty, which art, and wast, and art to come; because thou hast taken to thee thy great power, and hast reigned." Look at what happens at the sounding of the seventh or LAST trumpet. The kingdoms of this world become those of Christ Jesus. Obviously, what is being explained here by John is the return of Jesus and His coming to rule and reign for the Millennium.

One can see by reading what the Bible says and not what the doctrine of men says, that the Messiah will

come after the Tribulation and not before. He will come
and take those who have survived the Great Tribulation
away from the earth before God's judgment on "The Great
and Terrible Day of the Lord." So take heed and be ready
for what is ahead. Be like the assembly of Philadelphia
who survives the Tribulation not Smyrna who perishes.

*Special thanks are extended to the author's sister, Jane McKee,
for permission to reproduce this article. This paper was originally
written in 1996 as a middle school persuasive paper at the Christian
academy Jane was attending. Although she was given an A+ and
commended for her ability to prove her thesis, she was nevertheless
censured and unable to share it with her fellow students because it
conflicted with the views of the school.*

Introduction

The report you are about to examine has been composed to address some doctrinal problems—and perhaps some serious spiritual issues—among various Believers today. Many are of the position that any moment, perhaps in the next sixty seconds, Yeshua the Messiah (Jesus Christ) can come and rapture us all to Heaven prior to the Tribulation period. This belief, known as **the pre-tribulation rapture**, is extremely popular among those of our generation.

All too often, those who do not agree with pre-tribulationism can be, at the very least, branded as being misguided. However, in some circles, such people can be considered heretics, denying one of the (*supposed*) principal beliefs of Biblical faith. It is imperative that while we recognize that one's position on the timing of the return of the Lord is *not* a salvation issue, those of us not holding to pre-tribulationism must address why we believe it is flawed. We must answer the claims made in support of the pre-tribulation rapture from Scripture in a fair and reasonable manner, which pre-tribulationists have a strong tendency to not often demonstrate toward many post-tribulationists.

My personal testimony of not believing in the pre-tribulation rapture is somewhat unique. I attended a fundamentalist independent Baptist elementary school in my early years, so when the subject of the end-times came up, we were simply taught to believe in the pre-tribulation rapture. Any deviation from this belief (or even from the King James Version) was considered dangerous, or perhaps even cultish. This may have been the exception, as in many denominations and churches the end-times would not be considered that important, but it was my experience. The end-times were always exciting to me, and I always wondered why I felt a deep fascination with the prophetic Scriptures, especially since we were not supposed to be here during the Tribulation but be raptured up to Heaven. Several years later when I entered into high school, I was exposed to alternative views that I had never heard before, and I began to question whether or not the pre-tribulation rapture had the validity which many gave to it. My salvation experience in 1995 had led me to conclude that since God was powerful enough to deliver me from all the sin and some various demonic forces that had been influencing me, certainly He could protect us through the prophesied Tribulation period.[a]

As a new Believer I began a process of reading through one chapter of the Gospels every morning. I started with the Gospel of Matthew, and was enriched by being able to simply sit down and meditate on the text. Within the first month of doing this I got to Matthew 24, the Messiah's Olivet Discourse on the Last Days. The verses which caught my attention, in a morning quiet time, were Matthew 24:29-31:

> "Immediately after the distress of those days 'the sun will be darkened, and the moon will not give its light; the stars will fall from the sky, and the heavenly bodies will be shaken.' At that time the sign of the Son of Man will appear in the sky, and all the nations of the earth will mourn. They will see the Son of Man coming on the clouds of the sky, with power and great glory. And he will send his angels with a loud trumpet call, and they will gather his elect from the four winds, from one end of the heavens to the other" (NIV).

Perhaps you have read these same verses before, and have wondered...

---

[a] This is discussed, in part in Chapter 13 of the author's book *Introduction to Things Messianic*, "The Assurance of Our Salvation," and his publication *Why Hell Must Be Eternal*.

Having read that Yeshua (Jesus) would gather the saints "after the distress of those days" in the NIV, I started comparing this text with some other Bible versions that I had convenient. I had been accustomed to using the King James Version in elementary school, and it confirmed my suspicions, saying that the Messiah returned "Immediately after the tribulation of those days."

This was the first time I had ever really examined what the Scriptures told me about the timing of "the rapture." I had never known that our Lord Himself plainly said He was going to gather the saints after the Tribulation, and not before it as I had been taught. I began to get my hands on as much information pertaining to "the rapture debate" that a 14-year old could find. Two books that really helped me formulate some early opinions, which my stepfather had contributed to our new family's library, were George Eldon Ladd's *The Blessed Hope* (Grand Rapids: Eerdmans, 1956) and *The Church and the Tribulation* by Robert H. Gundry (Grand Rapids: Eerdmans, 1973). Both of these works are considered "classics" in this debate, representing post-tribulationism. I also consulted some popular pre-tribulational works, as the *Left Behind* series of prophecy novels was just starting to be released, and a popular fiction book which had preceded it was *The Third Millennium* (Nashville: Thomas Nelson, 1993) by Paul Meier. While I was intrigued by the debate between pre- and post-tribulationists, I found myself moving more and more toward the post-tribulational position. I was eager to discuss it with people I knew.

When I shared my newly found convictions with my peers, most rejected it. Many told me that they could not believe that God would ever make them go through the Tribulation, especially as they were planning to get married, have children, and start careers. God, in their words, would never "ruin their plans." God would never make them experience the horrors of the Last Days, including the possibility of being martyred for the faith. To them, the Lord would simply return unexpectedly to take them to Heaven for a big "surprise party." I was very shocked by these attitudes, because one with true faith in God should expect Him to provide total protection and guidance through whatever hardships life has to offer. *True Biblical faith is not about "fun and games" at all.* True commitment to the Lord requires sacrifices, and the Second Coming of Yeshua the Messiah is by no means some "surprise party." (Furthermore, all that one really needs in life are food, clothing, and shelter.)[b]

I found the attitudes of my peers to be unacceptable. But, most of their words were simply immature and indicative of those who lacked life experience, yet perhaps among a few they were words of outright rebellion toward God. The responses I received as I was "entertaining" post-tribulationism were disconcerting and very disturbing. The escapist, "partying" attitude I encountered from the "next generation" of Christians was one of the reasons that finally pushed me over the edge to renouncing a belief in the pre-tribulation rapture. It was also at this same time that my family was investigating a local Messianic Jewish congregation. In 1996, we fully entered into the Messianic movement, and for me personally, becoming Messianic is very closely connected with me becoming a post-tribulationist. And as my loving sister Jane will half-jokingly observe, "Being Messianic and a pre-tribulationist is a contradiction in terms. It will cause someone to spontaneously combust!"

My life's testimony has been one where God continually has "ruined," or more appropriately has altered, my personal plans. I would certainly not be writing this unless the Lord has put me through some trials and tribulations that have been influential in molding me as a person and have given me the strong faith that I have. In 1992, my father Kimball McKee died of melanoma, a deadly form of skin cancer that he had for only five months.[c] In 1994, my mother was remarried and

---

[b] 1 Timothy 6:8.
[c] A biographical sketch of Kim McKee is available as part of the K. Kimball McKee Memorial Fund <outreachisrael.net/kkm-fund.html>,

I was transplanted from my home of 14 years in the Northern Kentucky/Greater Cincinnati area to Dallas, Texas. Between 1994 and 1997 I attended four schools, because we moved around in the Dallas area, but it was hardly an ideal experience for someone trying to get established. In 1998, our family lived in the Bay Islands of Honduras for eight months to assist with a missionary endeavor. While there we experienced the deadly Hurricane Mitch. This is only a short list of various trials which I have experienced, but I would add to this that anyone who has been in full time ministry can tell you that trials and challenges *inevitably come with the job.*

I cannot agree with the assessment that God would not put us into difficult circumstances, including the Tribulation period. The Prophet Isaiah says, "when Your judgments are wrought on earth, the inhabitants of the world learn righteousness. But when the scoundrel is spared, he learns not righteousness" (Isaiah 26:9-10, NJPS). Through trials, we learn what the righteousness and holiness of God are all about, and we get to realize how much we need to rely on Him and be separated from the sinful world around us. Many of the First Century Believers in Yeshua the Messiah experienced persecutions, distresses, and even martyrdom. **They endured trials that we cannot hope to imagine.** Who are we to think that we are better than they? Who are we to think that we are better than those who walked and talked with Yeshua or His original Disciples? What gives us the right to be so presumptuous?

As editor of the Biblical news website TNN Online (www.tnnonline.net), the Theology News Network, an endeavor started in 1997, I am continually facing trials. This website today addresses a substantial amount of controversial views that I receive criticism for—much of it being unfair and unwarranted criticism. Some of this criticism comes from those in the Christian community,

---

with donations accepted by Outreach Israel Ministries, specifically established so that his Christian friends and associates can help to see his ministry work continue via his surviving family.

---

and some of it actually comes from those in the very Messianic community I serve. As if that were not enough, my college experience at the University of Oklahoma from 1999-2003 had its fair share of negativity from Christians on campus who did not understand my Messianic beliefs and Torah obedience, nor gave me ample ability to speak and explain myself. Some of my Christian peers—once again—felt that it was more appropriate to insult and berate me rather than to search the Scriptures for answers and seek reasoned and polite dialogue. I hold no ill feelings, but I have faced my fair share of difficulty from those "of the faith."

Aside from the fact that the Lord will obviously put us through hard times, comes the required analysis of the popular doctrine known as the pre-tribulation rapture. Is it valid? Or does it have a shaky foundation? *The Dangers of Pre-Tribulationism* is intended to respond to many of the reasons why people believe in the pre-tribulation rapture. I intend to demonstrate to you why these reasons are flawed, are often based on a poor reading of the Scriptures, and in some cases I will expose the escapist agenda of its proponents. This report has been written as a supplement to my book *When Will the Messiah Return?* By necessity, various points discussed in *When Will the Messiah Return?* will be reemphasized in this analysis, and there is overlap between the two publications. However, it is still advised and recommended that you have read *When Will the Messiah Return?* before reading *The Dangers of Pre-Tribulationism.*

The Dangers of Pre-Tribulationism was originally written as an article on the TNN Online website in 1999, which addressed the top twelve reasons why people believe in the pre-tribulation rapture. Many readers considered this article, at the time, to perhaps be the most provocative, compelling, and controversial article on the entire website. This report has taken and expanded that article, addressing many more reasons. It shows why believing in the pre-tribulation rapture can be dangerous and why it must be reevaluated and tested against Scripture.

It is my hope and prayer that this will prove to be a guide for many of you who are seeking a fuller understanding of the end-times, and a more Biblically sound eschatology. For those of you who have already seen some of the errors of the pre-tribulation rapture, this will be an excellent resource for you to use when encountering staunch pre-tribulationists. This treatise will reinforce what you already know to be true. For those of you who are pre-tribulationists, I encourage you to reevaluate your view and see if it really is Scripturally valid, as it will be seriously challenged and decompiled.

It is not the purpose of this publication to "blast" or condemn pre-tribulationists by any means, but rather force people to reevaluate the pre-tribulation rapture teaching. **Please understand that I do not consider pre-tribulationists to be "unsaved" because of their view.** But is their view truly taught in the Bible? Or is it popular, because it is unscriptural and escapist? These are some questions that I ask you to keep in mind throughout your reading. It is my intention to answer the pre-tribulation rapture claims reasonably, and with love and humility as demonstrated to us by the actions of Messiah Yeshua and His Apostles, as well as with a fairness that is often not given to post-tribulationists.

J.K. McKee
Editor, TNN Online

◾**1**◾

The Messiah Will Return

The issues surrounding what many call "the rapture" and its timing have caused much unnecessary debate, slander, and criticism over the years in evangelical Christianity. People from all the various views surrounding the gathering of the Lord's own unto Himself have at times slandered one another, and in many cases, have given eschatology, or the study of end things, an overall bad name. To those of us who believe in reasoned discussion rather than fierce debate, this is of some concern. While in mainstream and popular Christianity, the pre-tribulation rapture position is often overwhelmingly represented in comparison to post-tribulationism, the numbers are much more even in the Messianic movement. We should strive for an ample position so that we might examine this subject fairly, rationally, and above all Scripturally.

We are commanded by the Bible to "Be diligent to present yourself approved to God as a workman who does not need to be ashamed, accurately handling the word of truth" (2 Timothy 2:15). We are also told to be "diligent to preserve the unity of the Spirit in the bond of peace" (Ephesians 4:3). Yeshua the Messiah (Jesus Christ) tells us quite plainly, "By this all men will know that you are My disciples, if you have love for one another" (John 13:35). When we critique others for what they believe concerning an issue like this, it must be tempered in a generous spirit of fairness. It must be done constructively so we can all gain something from the discussion, and if necessary change, or at least fine-tune, our theological beliefs. The issue surrounding the return of Yeshua is very important as far as our overall theology should be concerned. After His ascension into Heaven, the angels present attested, "Men of Galilee, why do you stand looking into the sky? This Yeshua, who has been taken up from you into heaven, will come in just the same way as you have watched Him go into heaven" (Acts 1:11). Without any doubt, the Messiah will return. As the Apostles' Creed states concerning Yeshua: "[He] ascended into heaven and sitteth at the right hand of the Father whence he cometh to judge the living and the dead."[1] **Regardless of our view, we must be united around the common hope that our Lord will come back as has been foretold.**

The primary concern surrounding the return of the Messiah for pre-millennialists—those who believe that Yeshua returns before His thousand-year Millennial reign—has never really been the event itself and what the resurrection involves,[2] but rather its timing. It is the most debated topic between those who study prophecy today, and will continue to be until He returns.

It must be said that one's position on the return of the Messiah does not necessarily have to have a bearing on where he or she spends eternity. This does not have to be a "salvation issue," as some individuals at times make it out to be.[3] But, there are concerns that should exist when

---

[1] Henry Bettenson and Chris Maunder, eds., *Documents of the Christian Church* (Oxford: Oxford University Press, 1999), 26.

[2] Many of the specifics of this will be analyzed in the author's forthcoming publication, *The Resurrection and the Age to Come.*

[3] Pre-tribulationists Todd Strandberg and Terry James, *Are You Rapture Ready?* (New York: Dutton, 2003), 49, rightly acknowledge that the debate over "rapture timing" is not a salvation issue:

"No other doctrinal issue brings about more uproar in Christian ranks than do differences in belief about the Rapture. Many arguments

a person gets too comfortable or too dogmatic with an opinion surrounding events that are *yet to occur.* We must be open to alternatives if the end-times do not play out exactly as we expect. We have to all recognize that whatever position we hold to, pre-tribulational or post-tribulational, that we are dealing with future events. Our end-time charts may not necessarily "pan out" as we think they will.

I am very explicit about my views, and do not wish any of you to be confused about what I *might believe.* I take the Scriptures at face value for what they say and believe in a literal return of Yeshua the Messiah (Jesus Christ) to Planet Earth. I believe that there will be a physical removal of the saints from Planet Earth prior to His touchdown upon the Mount of Olives (Zechariah 14:4). I affirm that a seven-year period known as the Seventieth Week of Israel will occur, with its latter half being known as the Great Tribulation (Daniel 9:27; cf. Matthew 24:21; Mark 13:19). During this time of intense horrors, the Scriptures tell us that many millions of people on this planet will die, many of whom will unfortunately be eternally condemned. I affirm orthodox Biblical truths that have sustained our faith since the time of the Apostles and were restored during the Protestant Reformation. And most importantly for you to note, I am a Messianic Believer who strongly emphasizes the Hebraic Roots of our faith and the Torah obedient lifestyle adhered to by Yeshua (Jesus) and His Jewish Disciples.[4]

Now that you know something of my theological basis, it is important that we address the issues

---

over that event divide Christians who otherwise agree almost right down the line on crucial doctrines, such as those involving salvation."

[4] If you are unfamiliar with any of the ideas or concepts concerning the Messianic movement and the Hebraic Roots of the faith, consult the workbook *Hebraic Roots: An Introductory Study* co-written by the author and William Mark Huey, and the author's book *Introduction to Things Messianic.*

Also consult the author's book *The New Testament Validates Torah* and his publication *One Law for All.*

surrounding the Messiah's return. As the world gets more and more unstable, and with the Twenty-First Century fully upon us, many Believers are expecting Yeshua to come at any moment. *People are definitely talking about prophecy.* Within pre-millennial eschatology, the specific debate that exists is whether or not Yeshua will return **before or after** Daniel's Seventieth Week, also called the Tribulation period.

By far, the most popular of these two positions is that the Messiah will take the saints into Heaven prior to the Tribulation period (the full seven years) and then physically return to Earth at the close of the Great Tribulation. This is commonly referred to as the **pre-tribulation rapture** view, and is the one that many are familiar with today. The converse position is the **post-tribulation rapture** belief, in which the Messiah will gather Believers near, or at the end of, the Tribulation period, and then return to judge the world. This is the view which Outreach Israel Ministries and TNN Online holds to.[5]

We *do not* consider the issue of the rapture and Second Coming of Yeshua to be one of salvation, even though some pre-tribulationists I have encountered might consider it to be a salvation issue. *As a future event, it is open to interpretation.* However, it is our job as Believers to rightly search the Scriptures and be on guard when it pertains to His return. Yeshua Himself asks, "when the Son of Man comes, will He find faith on the earth?" (Luke 18:8). We are to be on alert when it pertains to His return, standing true in our faith in Him, and not give in to any populist interpretations. What we believe needs to be legitimately supported from God's Word and be

---

[5] Another belief similar to the post-tribulation perspective is the **pre-wrath** rapture, which many regard to be a "modified" form of post-trib. This publication is really not intended to debate the nuanced differences between the post-tribulation and pre-wrath rapture views, although we do emphasize that just like the pre-wrath rapture advocates, we believe that the saints are *indeed* spared from the wrath (Grk. *orgē*, ὀργή) of God.

consistent with the ideology we see beginning in the Torah, and upheld by the Prophets.

In this study, we will examine some of the common arguments given in reference for a pre-tribulation rapture escape. This is not intended to be the "final word" on the pre- versus post-trib rapture debate, as there are many other issues which surround it,[6] some of which will only be addressed in passing. But, I certainly hope that this analysis will demonstrate many of the shortcomings of the pre-tribulational belief system and reveal how unscriptural it really is. Most importantly, this report is written from a distinct Messianic viewpoint, so you may want to take serious note of how we feel about the rapture controversy, as opposed to us just being your average evangelical Christians. We are very concerned with the testimony of today's Messiah followers to both Israel and the worldwide Jewish community. We have a unique vantage point because we consider ourselves participants in the end-time restoration of Israel, and not part of a separate "Church" entity.

The intent of this analysis is to address some of the common reasons that most pre-tribulationists give for believing that Yeshua will gather His elect prior to the Tribulation. I hope you will find these reasons responded to fairly, as well as thoroughly. Even more important than this, we will be addressing the issues that surround those who hold *very strongly or militantly* to pre-tribulationism, perhaps making it an issue of salvation or fellowship. Is it a salvation issue, or is it an issue of interpretation? If the pre-tribulation rapture does not occur as so many Christians believe, what will they—*or perhaps even you*—do? **Are you really prepared for whatever may take place?**

---

[6] Many useful thoughts are available in Gleason L. Archer, Jr., and Paul D. Feinberg, Douglas J. Moo, Richard R. Reiter, *Three Views on the Rapture* (Grand Rapids: Zondervan, 1996), where these different scholars critique the others' point of view.

THE TOP REASONS PEOPLE BELIEVE IN THE PRE-TRIB RAPTURE

The following is a list of twelve common reasons why many people believe in the pre-tribulation rapture. These reasons are those which have been most commonly given to us by TNN Online website readers over the years who are pre-tribulationists. Their order primarily indicates the frequency of us hearing these arguments. As you should notice, some of the reasons listed seem somewhat absurd, some pose legitimate theological questions, and others pose some serious concern regarding the character of our Heavenly Father as He is perceived by some people.

"I BELIEVE IN THE PRE-TRIBULATION RAPTURE OUT OF RESPECT FOR MY PASTOR/BIBLE TEACHER."

The Holy Scriptures are replete with admonitions to respect others, and specifically those in positions of spiritual authority. Whether appointed by God or other humans, these persons do not deserve harsh, merciless, or unfair criticism. However, it is very important that we all recognize that a pastor, congregational leader, or even a highly respected theologian or teacher at a seminary, is a human being and will make mistakes. As James the Just admonishes, pertaining to Biblical teachers, "we will incur a stricter judgment" (James 3:1)—and I certainly take this warning very, very seriously. Teachers need to understand that what they say will affect others' opinions about God, His Word, and serious life decisions will often be made from what they say. They need to be very careful to not say any flippant thoughts or imperative statements in the context of instructing others from the Scriptures, but instead communicate things fairly and with an inquisitive tenor seeking truth.

A TNN Online reader once told me a story about one of his pastors who was fond of saying, "Do as I say but not as I do." It was later unfortunately discovered that he was having an extra-marital affair, and consequently many he was responsible for were seriously disturbed in their personal faith. He was forced to resign his position and he later ended up marrying the woman with whom he had been adulterating. Each one of us needs to take this kind of example to serious heart and understand that human teachers or pastors will always fail us (even if just on minor things), and look to *the Teacher*, Messiah Yeshua, for our ultimate answers.

Yeshua accused the leaders of the Pharisees of doing similar things (Matthew 23:1-11). On the outside these individuals showed a form of godliness, yet they were hypocritical as the Lord called them "whitewashed tombs" (Matthew 23:27). The Messiah did not issue a rebuke against all Pharisees, but certainly against those who had abused their power and position. Are there not religious leaders today who fit this same category? Do we not see those who profess some form of godliness, but do exactly the opposite? One of Yeshua's major rebukes to the Pharisaical leaders of His time was "They tie up heavy burdens and lay them on men's shoulders, but they themselves are unwilling to move them with *so much as a finger*" (Matthew 23:4). While they were willing to take all the credit for being "pious," they were unwilling to do some of the major work of serving others, making the required sacrifice.

Today, many pastors and leaders are embracing the ecumenical wave sweeping through our faith, in which key doctrines such as salvation coming only through

Yeshua the Messiah (Jesus Christ) or the final authority of Scripture, are being denied for the sake of "unity." As we should all recall from the Bible, true unity comes from individuals bound together in the Holy Spirit (cf. Ephesians 4:2-6) **and not** an edict from an ecumenical assembly or church council. Unfortunately, some pastors whose rapture position is pre-tribulational believe that it is acceptable for "unity" to occur with an apostate Roman Catholicism, many of whose members have given the Virgin Mary co-redeemer status with the Lord Jesus. While it is one thing to reach out to those of other religious groups, in an effort to show them a better way—it is another thing to join with them and look beyond some of their severe shortcomings.

Believing in any teaching or doctrine simply because someone you respect believes it can be dangerous. Pastors or Bible teachers are *human beings with flaws*, which we all must recognize. Placing one's complete trust and confidence in a human person will only bring harm. As the Apostle Peter warned how "there will also be false teachers among you, who will secretly introduce destructive heresies, even denying the Master who bought them, bringing swift destruction upon themselves" (2 Peter 2:1). By all means Bible teachers who commit their lives to a study of God's Word should be consulted and considered, but their conclusions must always be tested against God's Word.

The warning to watch out for false teachers in the Last Days is very real. Is believing in the pre-tribulation rapture doctrine—or any other Biblical doctrine for that matter—solely on the basis that someone whom you respect believes it, Biblically valid? **No.** You can respect a person for his or her position, but at the same time disagree based on Scripture in a civil manner. If you believe in any teaching solely on the basis of respecting someone, you need to pray and ask the Lord for Him to show you a better way of making theological conclusions. You need to ask Him to impart you with the ability to read the Bible better yourself, and give you the reasoning ability and discernment to deal with complicated issues.

"I BELIEVE IN THE PRE-TRIBULATION RAPTURE BECAUSE IT IS THE TRADITIONAL VIEW."

The issue surrounding the history of the pre-tribulation rapture is very intriguing. Very few are aware that the modern basis for the pre-tribulation rapture probably stems from the so-called visions of Scottish girl Margaret MacDonald in the 1830s, who claimed that God would give His people a "secret rapture" before the end-times. British theologian John Nelson Darby and the Plymouth Brethren movement later popularized beliefs based on her visions, and by the end of the Nineteenth Century dispensationalism began to be developed by theologians such as Cyrus Scofield. Sometimes, though, pre-tribulationists will quote figures from the early Church such as Pseudo-Ephraim from as early as 300 C.E., claiming that God would "rescue" His people before the Tribulation.

Certainly, while tradition should be a component in determining theology, believing in something because it is "traditional" can be problematic. During the Counter Reformation, many Catholic theologians argued against the Protestant Reformers solely on the basis that they went outside the authority of the pope and the traditions established by the papacy. The primary basis of any doctrine needs to be in the Bible itself, and frequently one *may* find a teaching confirmed by the historical record, as well as secondary and tertiary literature. Interestingly enough, however, John F. Walvoord, often considered to be the "dean" of pre-tribulationists, wrote that "posttribulationism, as far as the church as a whole is concerned, is the majority view."[1] Of course, it should also be noted that Walvoord *included* in this statement those of non pre-millennial views such as post-millennialism and amillennialism. However, notable great preachers, such as Charles Spurgeon, admired

---

[1] John F. Walvoord, *The Rapture Question* (Grand Rapids: Zondervan Publishing House, 1956), 127.

today   by   many   pre-tribulationists,   were   post-tribulational.[2]

Author Dave MacPherson has written a number of books detailing the history of the pre-tribulation rapture, including: *The Incredible Cover Up*, *The Rapture Plot*, and *The Three R's: Rapture, Revisionism, Robbery*. I agree with many of his conclusions, although I would leave the historical   argument   for   post-tribulationism   to MacPherson and others. Rather, our analyses in this publication are more concerned with the contours of theology and Biblical examination.

What is most important in this regard is really establishing if the "traditional" view is Biblically accurate. For almost 1,200 years, the Roman Catholic Church   was   virtually   the   only   representation   of Christianity in Western Europe—so if we are basing all of our theology solely on tradition, *Catholicism wins*. Early Reformers such as John Wycliffe, and later individuals such as William Tyndale, Martin Luther, Ulrich Zwigli, and John Calvin began the Reformation which changed the face of our faith. As they questioned unscriptural Catholic teaching, so might we question the popular pre-tribulation rapture doctrine.[3]

Many unfortunately believe in the pre-tribulation rapture on the basis that it has been the standard view for centuries in the past. In Mark 7:8-9, Messiah Yeshua told the Pharisees present that the primary reason that they rejected Him as the prophesied Deliverer was because they preferred their tradition over the teachings of Moses:

---

[2] The article, "Charles H. Spurgeon and Eschatology: Did He Have a   Discernible   Millennial   Position?",   available   for   access   via <http://spurgeon.org>, is a good summary of Spurgeon's post-tribulational position.

[3] In a similar vein, Outreach Israel Ministries and TNN Online will question some mainline Christian views in relation to the validity of the Torah, the seventh-day Sabbath, the Biblical appointments of Leviticus 23, and the kosher dietary laws of Scripture, *not* believing that such things were "done away with" by Messiah Yeshua. While not salvation issues, they do possess great benefits when practiced as a matter of a Believer's growth in holiness.

"'Neglecting the commandment of God, you hold to the tradition of men.' He was also saying to them, 'You are experts at setting aside the commandment of God in order to keep your tradition.'" As the Messiah also attested, "if you believed Moses, you would believe Me, for he wrote about Me" (John 5:46). Unfortunately, for many of the Pharisees, they considered their traditions to be so important that it would at times negate Scripture. When Yeshua arrived many of them could not see Him as the living Word of God. Certain Pharisees meticulously looked for *their tradition* to be kept by Him and could not find it. This is not to say that Yeshua did not keep many of the mainline traditions of His day, but He did not keep tradition at the expense of the Law of Moses itself, especially its weightier matters of ethics and morality.[4]

In a similar manner, the same instance has happened within much of Christianity concerning the pre-tribulation rapture. Because many people are taught this doctrine in church and fail to question its validity and examine it from the Scriptures first, they accept it as being legitimate. If the issue for you is tradition versus the Bible, which do you choose? *We would hope you choose the Holy Scriptures.* There are too many varied traditions regarding the end-times for tradition to be the sole determining factor in what to believe about the Messiah's return. We have to instead root our main conclusions within the Biblical text.

---

[4] The issue of how much or how little of the First Century Jewish customs and traditions Yeshua actually kept is a great matter of scholarly debate. It requires us to look at each instance in the Gospels of His encounters with the Pharisees, or His interactions with fellow Jews, and consider the historical background as detailed in the Rabbinical literature and other available data from the time. While Yeshua may appear to be criticizing the Pharisees in many instances, it may be only a particular group of Pharisees such as the School of Hillel or the School of Shammai.

Consult the author's article "You Want to Be a Pharisee," for a summary of these issues.

"I BELIEVE IN THE PRE-TRIBULATION RAPTURE BECAUSE WE CANNOT KNOW THE TIME OF THE MESSIAH'S RETURN."

Those who claim that Yeshua can return at any moment primarily base this on His words, "But of that day and hour no one knows, not even the angels of heaven, nor the Son, but the Father alone" (Matthew 24:36; cf. Mark 13:32). Yet is this truly a legitimate basis for what some call the doctrine of imminence? No. All that the Messiah says is that no one knows the day or the hour, meaning *the exact time* of His return. Is He saying that He can return at any moment? Consider the fact that much of Yeshua's Olivet Discourse on the Last Days is spent explaining the general signs that His followers are to look for that lead to His return, including: wars, famines, terrible Earth changes, and ultimately the Abomination of Desolation. If certain events are to precede the coming of the Lord, then He cannot return at any moment.

The Apostle Paul writes, "Now as to the times and the epochs, brethren, you have no need of anything to be written to you. For you yourselves know full well that the day of the Lord will come just like a thief in the night. While they are saying, 'Peace and safety!' then destruction will come upon them suddenly like labor pains upon a woman with child, and they will not escape. But you, brethren, are not in darkness, that the day would overtake you like a thief" (1 Thessalonians 5:1-4).

The specific saying that is frequently given to support the so-called imminent return of the Messiah is where Paul claims, "For you yourselves know full well that the day of the Lord will come just like a thief in the night (1 Thessalonians 5:2). However, in this same passage, Paul also clarifies that at this time "While people are saying, 'Peace and safety,' destruction will come on them suddenly, as labor pains on a pregnant woman, and they will not escape" (1 Thessalonians 5:3, NIV). He further writes, "But you, brethren, are not in darkness, that the day would overtake you like a thief" (1

Thessalonians 5:4). There is no allusion in 1 Thessalonians 5:1-4 to any removal of Believers. Rather, this passage speaks of the sudden judgment of God upon the world and our collective need as His people to be on guard.

Another important passage to note is 2 Peter 3:10-12:

"But the day of the Lord will come like a thief, in which the heavens will pass away with a roar and the elements will be destroyed with intense heat, and the earth and its works will be burned up. Since all these things are to be destroyed in this way, what sort of people ought you to be in holy conduct and godliness, looking for and hastening the coming of the day of God, because of which the heavens will be destroyed by burning, and the elements will melt with intense heat!"

The Apostle Peter says that on the Day of the LORD, *which comes as a thief*, that "the heavens will pass away with a great noise" (KJV) and that "the earth and the works that are upon it will be burned up" (RSV). Again, there is no allusion to any rapture, but rather of God's judgment upon Planet Earth.

Consider this: what does a thief come and do? A thief comes to steal from a person and utterly ruin him. A thief comes unexpectedly. 1 Thessalonians 5:4 admonishes Believers not to be ignorant so that the Day of the LORD would overtake them, imploring them to be on guard. Yeshua Himself warns, "if the householder had known at what time of night the burglar was coming, he would have kept awake and not have let his house be broken into. Hold yourselves ready, therefore, because the Son of Man will come at the time you least expect him" (Matthew 24:43-44, NEB). How can we compare the Second Coming of the Messiah to an unexpected break-in—and conclude that this break-in is a *good thing*? Do any of us want Yeshua to arrive as though He were a burglar—or do we want to be ready at all times so we are not caught unaware?

The warnings of Scripture should remain true to us every day, and whether or not Yeshua returns in our lifetime, we need to be on guard and ready as though He will return. **We do not need to find ourselves derelict in the work that He has given us to perform.** Yeshua says in the Book of Revelation, "Behold, I am coming like a thief. Blessed is the one who stays awake and keeps his clothes, so that he will not walk about naked and men will not see his shame" (Revelation 16:15). None of us should ever want the Messiah to show up so unexpectedly that we find ourselves "shamefully exposed" (NIV).

Furthermore, if we believe that Yeshua's actual gathering of the saints is to be post-tribulational, and Believers will have to endure the hardships of the Tribulation period, then we must consider the fact that it is prophesied that the world will be engulfed in a time of great darkness prior to Yeshua's advent. Prior to the Lord's appearing, Revelation 9:1-6 tells us that something is going to hit the Earth and that great smoke is going to blanket the planet. Locust creatures (whatever these may be or represent) will come forth to torment people, but this will only take place for a period of five months:

"Then the fifth angel sounded, and I saw a star from heaven which had fallen to the earth; and the key of the bottomless pit was given to him. He opened the bottomless pit, and smoke went up out of the pit, like the smoke of a great furnace; and the sun and the air were darkened by the smoke of the pit. Then out of the smoke came locusts upon the earth, and power was given them, as the scorpions of the earth have power. They were told not to hurt the grass of the earth, nor any green thing, nor any tree, but only the men who do not have the seal of God on their foreheads. And they were not permitted to kill anyone, but to torment for five months; and their torment was like the torment of a scorpion when it stings a man. And in those days men will seek death and will not find it; they will long to die, and death flees from them."

These locust creatures will have free reign to torment humans during these five months of darkness. Further descriptions of this time of almost total darkness appear in Revelation and the Book of Joel. In Revelation 6:12,

John the Apostle states, "I looked when He broke the sixth seal, and there was a great earthquake; and the sun became black as sackcloth *made* of hair, and the whole moon became like blood." This parallels the prophecies of Joel, who says that "The sun will be turned into darkness and the moon into blood before the great and awesome day of the LORD comes" (Joel 2:31). Describing the severity of this darkness, he proclaims that "The sun and moon grow dark and the stars lose their brightness" (Joel 3:15).

These prophecies describe the reality that a meteor or comet will hit the Earth, causing black clouds to engulf the atmosphere. A major side effect of this could be that Earth is thrown off of its axis, thus being responsible for any number of other great judgments of God in which He will inflict further devastation. While the text tells us that this darkness will be in place for five months, we must consider the chance that individual days may be reduced in length from twenty-four hours to a possible shorter length. This is because Yeshua tells us, "Unless the Lord had shortened *those* days, no life would have been saved; but for the sake of the elect, whom He chose, He shortened the days" (Mark 12:30). While "five months" will occur—it may be an accelerated five months.

The Messiah's assertion that He will return at a time that only the Father knows is true for us, because the time for humans living on Earth will have substantially changed in some way. Even those with watches during this time of darkness will be unable to actually know what "day" it is, because Planet Earth may very well be thrown off its axis in such a way that the "days" are shortened in length. *They will be unable to count off the days remaining.* How short they will be we can only speculate. Those living during this time will have to turn to God for their total provision, just as He preserved the Ancient Israelites during the darkness He inflicted upon the Egyptians in the time of the Exodus.

It is very true that no human being can know the *exact* time of our Lord's return, but this is not a legitimate basis to say that Yeshua can "return at any moment" for

Believers (although each one of us should be prepared to meet Him *personally* at all times, as we can die at any moment). Unfortunately for pre-tribulationists, none of the verses used to support the doctrine of imminence say that Yeshua can come for the corporate body of saints at any time. Rather, the admonitions which we see direct Messiah followers to be on guard and not be overtaken like a thief *or burglar* who is coming to steal and utterly ruin.

"I BELIEVE IN THE PRE-TRIBULATION RAPTURE BECAUSE THE MESSIAH WILL COME LIKE NOAH AND THE FLOOD."

In Matthew 24:37-39, Yeshua informed His Disciples, that the days prior to His return would be like the days of Noah:

"For the coming of the Son of Man will be just like the days of Noah. For as in those days before the flood they were eating and drinking, marrying and giving in marriage, until the day that Noah entered the ark, and they did not understand until the flood came and took them all away; so will the coming of the Son of Man be."

Similar to the faulty logic pertaining to pre-tribulationists claiming that the Messiah will come for them as a "thief in the night," a poor reading of this is also often applied by many pre-tribulationists regarding Yeshua's comparison of the days of Noah to the days prior to His return. Matthew 24:38-39 describes that people were "eating and drinking, marrying and giving in marriage…until the flood came and took them all away." Many would like us to believe that those taken away are representative of those who will be "taken" into the clouds, and into glory, when the Messiah returns.

When comparing this to the Noahdic Flood in Genesis ch. 6, those *taken away* were not at all "raptured." Noah was safe in the ark that the Lord instructed Him to build. When the floodwaters came, those who were not in the ark were killed by the floodwaters—they were *taken away*. The specific Greek verb translated "took" in Matthew 24:39, *airō* (αἴρω), means "*to take from among the living*, either by a natural death...or by violence" (*Thayer*).[5] Once Noah was safe inside the ark, the Flood came and swept everyone else away. In a similar sense, once Believers go to meet Yeshua in the clouds after the Tribulation, many who remain will be physically consumed by the wrath of God poured out upon Planet Earth (Isaiah 13:6-13; Malachi 4:1-3).

A similar support for the pre-tribulation rapture is given from Matthew 24:40-41, which says, "Then there will be two men in the field; one will be taken and one will be left. Two women *will be* grinding at the mill; one will be taken and one will be left." Again, many would like to imply that those taken are "raptured" up to Heaven. However, the Greek of this likewise does not support this premise. The verb translated "taken" in these two verses is *paralambanō* (παραλαμβάνω), which can relate to "the removal of persons from the earth in judgment, when 'the Son of Man is revealed'" (*Vine*).[6] As a verb, *paralambanō* does have varied usages which can only be determined by context, some of which are rather neutral, but a being "taken" to judgment is the theme here. *AMG* further observes,

"[I]n these verses, those who are taken are not to be misconstrued as those whom the Lord favors, as if they were the same saints spoken of in 1 Thes. 4:17 who will be raptured...to meet the Lord in the clouds. The verb *paralambánō* in most cases indicates a demonstration in favor of the one taken, but not always...It is used to refer to those in the days of Noah who were taken away, not being favored but being punished, while Noah and his family were left intact. Therefore, in this passage...*paralambánō* must not be equated to the believers who are to be raptured at the coming of the

---

[5] Joseph H. Thayer, *Thayer's Greek-English Lexicon of the New Testament* (Peabody, MA: Hendrickson, 2003), 17.

[6] W.E. Vine, *Vine's Expository Dictionary of New Testament Words* (Nashville: Thomas Nelson, 1980), 616.

Lord for His saints. It refers rather to those who, as in the days of Noah, are taken to destruction."[7]

This is quite different than the verb *analambanō* (ἀναλαμβάνω), which means "to take up" (*Vine*),[8] in reference to Yeshua's ascension on "the day when He was taken up [*analambanō*] to heaven" (Acts 1:2).

The Greek verb translated "left" in Matthew 24:40-41 is *aphiēmi* (ἀφίημι), generally meaning "*to let go, let alone, let be,*" or "*to disregard.*" It can also mean "*to remit, forgive*" (*Thayer*).[9] Some argue that those taken in Matthew 24:40-42 are *taken to judgment* and those "left" are simply *left alone*. Those left alone are mortals who enter into Yeshua's Millennial Kingdom. However, we should also note that *aphiēmi* can mean "To let go from one's further notice...to leave or let alone" (*AMG*),[10] so it may be "left" in a neutral context.

We know that the understanding of *paralambanō* as being taken to judgment is the correct interpretation per Luke's parallel account of Yeshua's words:

"There will be two women grinding at the same place; one will be taken and the other will be left. *Two men will be in the field; one will be taken and the other will be left.* And answering they said to Him, 'Where, Lord?' And He said to them, 'Where the body *is*, there also the vultures will be gathered'" (Luke 17:35-37).[11]

Yeshua said, in comparing the days of Noah to the time before His return, **for His followers to be on guard and on alert to His coming.** During the time of Noah, all of humanity with the exception of Noah's family was utterly evil. Noah and his family were saved from above

---

[7] Zodhiates, *The Complete Word Study Dictionary: New Testament*, 1108.

[8] *Vine*, 615.

[9] *Thayer*, 89.

[10] Zodhiates, *Complete Word Study Dictionary: New Testament*, 299.

[11] The same Greek verbs used in Matthew 24:35-37 for *taken* and *left, paralambanō* and *aphiēmi*, are used in this passage. For a further examination of this issue, consult Appendix A in *When Will the Messiah Return?*: "Is Being 'Taken' Always a Good Thing?"

the judgment (a type of the "rapture") and when they were in the ark, the Flood came and took—or *killed*—the rest (cf. 1 Peter 3:20; 2 Peter 2:5). The Flood did not "rapture people" to Heaven as many pre-tribulationists would like us to think the Lord is alluding to. Furthermore, the Flood only lasted forty days. If pre-tribulationists would like us to think that Noah was saved from the entire judgment, be rest assured that Noah was fully aware of the ecological disaster around him while in the ark. When Believers meet the Lord in the clouds, they will be aware that He pulled them out at the last minute, as the full brunt of His judgment will then be issued upon the Earth.

"I BELIEVE IN THE PRE-TRIBULATION RAPTURE BECAUSE WE ARE NOT APPOINTED TO GOD'S WRATH."

No one can deny the clear Biblical reference of 1 Thessalonians 5:9: "For God has not destined us for wrath, but for obtaining salvation through our Lord Yeshua the Messiah." Neither this, nor other passages such as Romans 5:9, should ever be in dispute by post-tribulationists. However, it is important that we determine **what** the wrath of God actually is, something very few pre-tribulationists often make the effort to do. Pre-tribulationists errantly consider the entire Tribulation period to be God's wrath.

There are two primary Greek words used in the Apostolic Scriptures translated as "wrath" in our English Bibles: *orgē* (ὀργή) and *thumos* (θυμός), each indicative of a particular type of wrath or anger of God.

BDAG defines *orgē* as "**strong indignation directed at wrongdoing, w. focus on retribution, wrath.**"[12] This is necessary to understand because it indicates that *orgē* "wrath" is most often reserved for the Divine punishment of God on sinners. *Thayer* adds to this, telling us that *orgē*

---

[12] *BDAG*, 720.

is indicative of *"anger exhibited in punishing*, hence used for the *punishment* itself."[13]

Thumos, on the other hand, is described as **"a state of intense displeasure, *anger, wrath, rage, indignation*"** *(BDAG)*.[14] *Thayer* remarks that it means *"passion, angry heat...anger forthwith boiling up and soon subsiding again."*[15] This does not indicate a "wrath" that is constant and steady, but one that is only momentary.

The comparison of these two terms is that *orgē* "denotes *indignation which has arisen gradually and becomes more settled" (Thayer)*.[16] *Orgē* is the Divine wrath used to describe the eternal punishment of unbelievers, whereas *thumos* is used to describe the anger of God poured out during the Tribulation period.

Interestingly enough, the only times the word *orgē* (Divine wrath) is used in the Book of Revelation are in a post-tribulational context (6:16, 17; 11:18; 14:10; 16:19; 19:15). It is used after the sixth seal (Revelation 6:16-17), the seventh (or the last) trumpet (Revelation 11:18), the seventh vial/bowl (Revelation 16:19), and is most importantly used to describe the eternal punishment of the condemned in the Lake of Fire (Revelation 14:10). Believers are indeed spared from the *orgē* wrath of God, as **(1)** the *orgē* or Divine wrath of God is poured out after the Tribulation period, and **(2)** the *orgē* of God is for those who reject the Messiah and suffer eternal punishment.

It should also be noted that numerous references exist throughout the Tanach or Hebrew Scriptures describing that the judgment of God is poured out on the Day of the LORD (i.e., Isaiah 13:6, 9; Ezekiel 30:3; 1:15; 2:1; 31; 3:14; Amos 5:18, 20; Obadiah 15; Zephaniah 1:14; Malachi 4:5). Although there are numerous interpretations that are given for the term "day," more often than not this can be used in reference to the point when Yeshua returns and defeats His enemies at

---

[13] *Thayer*, 452.
[14] *BDAG*, 461.
[15] *Thayer*, 293.
[16] Ibid.

Armageddon, initiating His Millennial reign. Presumably, before this Day of the LORD takes place, Believers have been removed from Planet Earth, because this judgment of God is reserved for the unrighteous.

The Apostolic Scriptures also speak of the Day of the LORD, which we should assume is likely the same event spoken of by the Prophets in the Tanach (cf. Acts 2:20; 1 Thessalonians 5:2; 2 Peter 3:10). The Word of God is clear that during this time period His wrath will be poured out.

But what do we really consider the "wrath" of God to be? Is the wrath of God just the Tribulation period? Here are some verses describing the wrath or *orgē* of God that need not escape our attention:

"For the wrath [*orgē*] of God is revealed from heaven against all ungodliness and unrighteousness of men who suppress the truth in unrighteousness...But because of your stubbornness and unrepentant heart you are storing up wrath [*orgē*] for yourself in the day of wrath [*orgē*] and revelation of the righteous judgment of God, who WILL RENDER TO EACH PERSON ACCORDING TO HIS DEEDS [Psalm 62:12; Proverbs 24:12]" (Romans 1:18; 2:5-6).

"But immorality or any impurity or greed must not even be named among you, as is proper among saints; and *there must be no* filthiness and silly talk, or coarse jesting, which are not fitting, but rather giving of thanks. For this you know with certainty, that no immoral or impure person or covetous man, who is an idolater, has an inheritance in the kingdom of Messiah and God. Let no one deceive you with empty words, for because of these things the wrath [*orgē*] of God comes upon the sons of disobedience. Therefore do not be partakers with them" (Ephesians 5:3-7).

The above passages from Romans 1:18, 2:4-6, and Ephesians 5:3-7 speak of wrath or *orgē* of God in regard to eternal damnation. *Thumos*, on the other hand, is indicative more of the *anger* of God, not always related to eternal punishment. In some instances, it is notable that *thumos* is also used to describe the wrath, the indignation or anger, of Satan. The following are a selection of quotations from the Book of Revelation where *thumos* is used:

"For this reason, rejoice, O heavens and you who dwell in them. Woe to the earth and the sea, because the devil has come down to you, having great wrath [*thumos*], knowing that he has *only* a short time" (Revelation 12:12).

"So the angel swung his sickle to the earth and gathered *the clusters from* the vine of the earth, and threw them into the great wine press of the wrath [*thumos*] of God. And the wine press was trodden outside the city, and blood came out from the wine press, up to the horses' bridles, for a distance of two hundred miles" (Revelation 14:19-20).

"Then I saw another sign in heaven, great and marvelous, seven angels who had seven plagues, *which are* the last, because in them the wrath [*thumos*] of God is finished" (Revelation 15:1).

In determining what the wrath of God actually encompasses, you need to be sure of what Greek term is used in the source text of the Apostolic Scriptures, and then compare the context of the passage. Ultimately, the "wrath" of God is rightfully considered to be eternal damnation, which all Believers—Tribulation saints or otherwise—will be spared from. However, once defining what the "wrath of God" actually is, and distinguishing the words *orgē* and *thumos*, we can then begin to address the more critical question: **Will Believers experience hard times?** This is a question that many pre-tribulationists answer incorrectly.

Many popular pre-tribulationists say, "Why would anyone want to go through the Tribulation?" None of us can blame them for asking this, because they would be correct as no one should want to go through the Tribulation. By no means is experiencing the Tribulation something one *should ever* wish for. If we post-tribulationists are wrong, and pre-tribulationists are right: *Praise God!*

But sadly, many pre-tribulationists prey on people's emotions rather than dealing with the facts that Believers in the Messiah have and will experience hard times—something American Christianity has never really had to face. We would be keen to heed the Prophet Isaiah's words: "I seek You with all the spirit within me. For when Your judgments are wrought on earth, the inhabitants of the world learn righteousness. But when the scoundrel is spared, he learns not righteousness" (Isaiah 26:9b-10a, NJPS). The judgment of God is to teach His people more about the holiness and righteousness of Him as our Creator.

"I BELIEVE IN THE PRE-TRIBULATION RAPTURE BECAUSE WE ARE SPARED FROM THE HOUR OF TESTING."

A popular reference used to support the premise that Believers are removed from Earth before the Tribulation period comes from Revelation 3:10, where Yeshua the Messiah promises to spare those of the congregation or assembly of Philadelphia from the hour of testing:

"Because you have kept my word about patient endurance, I will keep you from the hour of trial that is coming on the whole world, to try those who dwell on the earth" (ESV).

What is automatically assumed by most pre-tribulationists is that the congregation of Philadelphia comprises all Believers and that the "hour of testing" is the Tribulation period. This is a major interpretational problem. It is not appropriate to assume that all Believers in Yeshua somehow classify as being "Philadelphian," and furthermore that the "hour of testing" or "hour of trial" is the Tribulation period.

If we look at only a surface examination of who the Philadelphian Believers likely are, the Greek *Philadelphia* (Φιλαδελφία)—the name of a city in First Century Asia Minor—means *"brotherly love"* (*LS*),[17] a key indicator of

---

[17] H.G. Liddell and R. Scott, *An Intermediate Greek-English Lexicon* (Oxford: Clarendon Press, 1994), 657.

one of the spiritual characteristics that these people have. Revelation 3:10 says that the Philadelphians "have kept the word of My perseverance," with *hupomonē* (ὑπομονή) being "*a holding out, patient endurance*" (*LS*).[18] Yeshua issues a "command to endure" (HCSB) to the Philadelphians. Persevering in one's faith is not only remaining true to the teachings and commands of Scripture, accomplishing the Lord's tasks, but also regards how one *patiently waits* for the arrival of the Messiah.

Many people today are *most overanxious* in regard to the return of Yeshua and are not following the admonition of 2 Thessalonians 2:1-3, which says not to be disturbed in regard to the coming of the Lord. Through the advent of prophecy fiction books such as *Left Behind* and with pre-tribulationism indeed being promoted to an extreme, many people are **not** *patiently waiting* for the Messiah's return. Many are literally sitting on the edge of their seats waiting for an any-moment escape. Equally so, there are post-tribulationists preparing for the worst, storing up food, guns and ammunition, literally chomping at the bit for the Great Tribulation to begin—and who are most eager to read messages into current news.[19] Are such people—in both categories—*waiting patiently* for the Messiah's return? (How much has our own Messianic movement been plagued with various calculations and timetables regarding the Second Coming, all of which have kept us away from the day-to-day work of God's Kingdom?)

---

[18] Ibid., 845.

[19] One of the absolute worst, recent examples of this that I can consider is how some people in the Christian "prophecy world" (with more than a few Messianic adherents), actually promoted the idea that the Gulf of Mexico Deepwater Horizon oil spill disaster, which began on 20 April, 2010—as bad as it was for the economy and ecology of the Gulf Coast of the Southern United States—would *actually* kill a third of all sea life on Earth (cf. Revelation 8:9). And not only this, but others also promoted the idea that significant parts of the American coastline from Florida to Texas would be flooded underwater, after some kind of giant explosion, of which the oil spill was to only be a small part.

Those who belong to the true Philadelphian assembly have both brotherly love and are patient in regard to Yeshua's coming. They are patient because they are secure in the work of God's Kingdom on Planet Earth. **Not all who claim to have faith in the Messiah would classify as being "Philadelphian."** This is only a specific category of people.

The Greek term translated "testing" or "trial" in Revelation 3:10 is *peirasmos* (πειρασμός), which can be indicative of "the temptation by which the devil sought to divert Jesus the Messiah from his divine errand" (*Thayer*).[20] *TDNT* adds to this, "Rev. 3:10 promises deliverance in the final hour of trial."[21] The Messiah further tells those of the Philadelphian assembly, "He who overcomes, I will make him a pillar in the temple of My God, and he will not go out from it anymore; and I will write on him the name of My God, and the name of the city of My God, the new Jerusalem, which comes down out of heaven from My God, and My new name" (Revelation 3:12).

The testing that those of Philadelphia are preserved from is what will deter them from their calling: **to persevere.** In Matthew 4:1-11, Satan tempted Yeshua three times and the Lord responded to him with Holy Scripture. Had Yeshua worshipped the Devil, He would have been made king of the world, but would not have fulfilled His destiny as the Divine Redeemer. In a similar manner, we must prevail and have faith in Him— patiently waiting for His return. Many in the Tribulation period will be forced to either worship Satan or be martyred, and it is this form of "testing" from which I believe the Philadelphian Believers will be spared. They will be preserved from the temptation to fall away and apostatize. And, we would eagerly point out that this **does not include everyone.** Only a certain segment, who

---

[20] *Thayer*, 498.
[21] H. Sessemann, "test, attempt," in Geoffrey W. Bromiley, ed., *Theological Dictionary of the New Testament*, abridged (Grand Rapids: Eerdmans, 1985), 823.

God knows and specially calls out, will be spared from this temptation.

"I BELIEVE IN THE PRE-TRIBULATION RAPTURE BECAUSE THE HOLY SPIRIT MUST BE REMOVED FOR THE ANTICHRIST TO BE REVEALED."

Many pre-tribulationists believe that the antimessiah/antichrist can only be revealed after a "restrainer," or one who holds back, is removed. This restrainer is believed to be the Holy Spirit indwelling "the Church." When "the Church" has been raptured to Heaven, it is then believed that the man of lawlessness can be revealed. This is based on Paul's words in 2 Thessalonians 2:6-7:

"And you know what restrains him now, so that in his time he will be revealed. For the mystery of lawlessness is already at work; only he who now restrains *will do so* until he is taken out of the way."

This restrainer is commonly interpreted by pre-tribulationists to be the Holy Spirit. It is only when the Holy Spirit, they say, is removed via the rapture of the Church, that the Tribulation period can begin and the antimessiah can be revealed—supposedly as it is the Holy Spirit resident in the saints which is restraining Satan from taking control of the world.

We should find fault with this interpretation, primarily because the Book of Revelation speaks quite prominently of the Tribulation saints. These born again Believers without any doubt must have the Holy Spirit to have salvation. If the Holy Spirit is removed from Earth at this time, there can be no Tribulation saints—**for a true Believer must be regenerated by the Holy Spirit.** Those who would say that the Holy Spirit is removed for a short time and then "returns immediately" have no Scriptural support for their opinion.

The problem here lies in what the restrainer is. Who or what is presently holding back the full force of evil from being unleashed upon this planet? The restraining influence by no means has to be the Holy Spirit. Douglas J. Moo observes,

"[W]hatever one's view, it is improper to base very much on a text that is so notoriously obscure—the verb κατέχω [katcheō] can be translated 'hold back' or 'hold fast,' 'occupy,' and has been understood as signifying Rome/the emperor, civil government, God and His power, Michael the archangel, the preaching of the Gospel/Paul, Satan, general evil forces, a combination of benevolent forces, the Jewish state, and James, or a mythic symbol with no particular content."[22]

I quote Moo here to indicate that there are alternative viewpoints to believing that the restraining influence is something other than the Holy Spirit. The able interpreter should be able to decide which option is best, based on a comparison of corresponding passages.

Of those which have been proposed, we should consider how Daniel 12:1 tells us, "Now at that time Michael, the great prince who stands *guard* over the sons of your people, will arise. And there will be a time of distress such as never occurred since there was a nation until that time; and at that time your people, everyone who is found written in the book, will be rescued." This verse speaks of the Archangel Michael arising, and afterward a great time of "trouble" or "distress." The Hebrew noun is *tzarah* (צָרָה), rendered in the Septuagint as *thlipsis* (θλῖψις), the same word generally rendered in the Apostolic Scriptures as "tribulation." After Michael "arises," a time of Great Tribulation will befall God's people.

What is interesting about Daniel 12:1 is the context of this "standing up" by Michael. The verb *amad* (עָמַד) appears in the Qal stem (simple action, active voice), meaning "**take one's stand, stand**," in this instance relating to "*stand, be in a standing attitude*," or possibly even, "*take a stand* against...in opposition to" (*BDB*).[23] If the context of this verse has military implications, or at least implications regarding spiritual warfare, then when

---

[22] Douglas J. Moo, "The Case for the Posttribulation Rapture Position," in *Three Views on the Rapture*, 190.
[23] *BDB*, 763.

we examine Revelation 12:7-9, we see the position of Michael being the restrainer validated:

"And there was war in heaven, Michael and his angels waging war with the dragon. The dragon and his angels waged war, and they were not strong enough, and there was no longer a place found for them in heaven. And the great dragon was thrown down, the serpent of old who is called the devil and Satan, who deceives the whole world; he was thrown down to the earth, and his angels were thrown down with him."

The rising or standing up that occurs in Daniel 12:1 is the Archangel Michael making a military stand in Heaven against Satan and his forces. We are told that when Satan is cast out, "For this reason, rejoice, O heavens and you who dwell in them. Woe to the earth and the sea, because the devil has come down to you, having great wrath, knowing that he has *only* a short time" (Revelation 12:12). Both this, and the latter half of Daniel 12:1, are all too reminiscent of Yeshua's words in Matthew 24:21: "For then there will be great distress, unequaled from the beginning of the world until now—and never to be equaled again" (NIV).

Many evangelical Christians have recognized the possibility that Michael may be the restrainer. Unfortunately they have had no way to really counter the reality that he is "the great prince who champions your people" (Daniel 12:1, CJB), that people being Israel. Pre-tribulationists have said that Michael cannot be the restrainer because of the fact that he is not guarding "the Church," but only the Jewish people.

All Believers, be they Jewish or non-Jewish, have been made a part of the the Commonwealth of Israel (Ephesians 2:11-12) or the Israel of God (Galatians 6:16), being grafted-in to Israel's olive tree by faith in Israel's Messiah (Romans 11:16-17). The salvation of the nations is predicated on them being incorporated into an enlarged realm of Israel (cf. Acts 15:15-18; Amos 9:11-12). Presently, it is the Archangel Michael who is withholding Satan from unleashing the full force of evil upon us and upon this world—not the Holy Spirit.

"I BELIEVE IN THE PRE-TRIBULATION RAPTURE BECAUSE THE 'FALLING AWAY' OF 2 THESSALONIANS 2:3 IS THE RAPTURE."

I have observed that the defense offered from 2 Thessalonians 2:3—as it pertains to the "falling away" being the rapture—is primarily only used by what we might consider "hard core pre-tribulationists." As 2 Thessalonians 2:1-3 reads from the King James Version,

"Now we beseech you, brethren, by the coming of our Lord Jesus Christ, and *by* our gathering together unto him, That ye be not soon shaken in mind, or be troubled, neither by spirit, nor by word, nor by letter as from us, as that the day of Christ is at hand. Let no man deceive you by any means: for *that day shall not come*, except there come **a falling away first**, and that man of sin be revealed, the son of perdition."

Some think that this reference is speaking of the pre-tribulation rapture, even though it actually refers to the Second Coming or *parousia* when Yeshua comes to defeat His enemies.

Is the "falling away" the rapture? The Christian textbook *Book of Revelation, Church History, and Things to Come* states that "the Greek word translated *'falling away'* means *'departure, or going out,'* similar to our word *exit;* it refers to the rapture."[24] This is given as support for the pre-tribulation rapture. Her commentary continues, saying that "Some interpret *'falling away'* to mean apostasy (a departing from the faith), but the word *faith* is not in the text."[25]

What this textbook fails to do is actually tell us what this "mysterious Greek word" is, which just happens to be *apostasia* (ἀποστασία). The *Liddell-Scott* lexicon, primarily concerned with classical Greek, defines it as *"defection."*[26] BDAG says that it means **"defiance of established   system   or   authority,   *rebellion*,**

---

[24] Beka Horton, *Book of Revelation, Church History, and Things to Come* (Pensacola: Pensacola Christian College, 1993), 196.
[25] Ibid.
[26] *LS*, 107.

abandonment, breach of faith."[27] *Apostastia* is the root for our English word "apostasy," which itself means a rejection of or standing away from the faith. "Rebellion" is possibly another understanding, as the NIV renders 2 Thessalonians 2:3 with, "that day will not come until the **rebellion** occurs and the man of lawlessness is revealed."[28]

In my opinion, this is blatant manipulation on the part of this textbook's author, which is absolutely unacceptable when it pertains to proper Scripture interpretation.[29] The New American Standard Bible, a widely respected, modern evangelical Christian Bible translation, translates 2 Thessalonians 2:1-3 with "apostasy":

"Now we request you, brethren, with regard to the coming of our Lord Jesus Christ and our gathering together to Him, that you not be quickly shaken from your composure or be disturbed either by a spirit or a message or a letter as if from us, to the effect that the day of the Lord has come. Let no one in any way deceive you, for *it will not come* unless the **apostasy** comes first, and the man of lawlessness is revealed, the son of destruction" (2 Thessalonians 2:1-3).

We must consider the fact that many (perhaps most) modern Bible versions are translated by pre-tribulationists, or at least have a significant number of pre-tribulationists involved. If "departure" were a legitimate rendering of *apostasia*, then it would be employed as such.[30] None of the major, modern English

---

[27] *BDAG*, 120.

[28] Other notable usages of *apostasia* appear in Joshua 22:22; 2 Chronicles 29:19; and Jeremiah 2:19, and 1 Maccabees 2:15 in the Septuagint, and especially in Acts 21:21 where Paul was falsely accused of telling the Jews to "forsake Moses."

[29] Indeed, I would say that any writings, pre-trib, post-trib, or otherwise, which mention Hebrew or Greek "words" without specifically saying what they are, are being manipulative. Such methodologies in my opinion are unacceptable for any Biblical teaching.

[30] A term best meaning "departure" is *analusis* (ἀνάλυσις), appearing in 2 Timothy 4:6:

Bible versions render *apostasia* with anything close to "departure" in 2 Thessalonians 2:3. The Contemporary English Version has, "But don't be fooled! **People will rebel against God.** Then before the Lord returns, the wicked one who is doomed to be destroyed will appear," and the New Living Translation renders it with "that day will not come until there is **a great rebellion against God** and the man of lawlessness is revealed." The terms "rebel against" (CEV) or "great rebellion" (NLT) are a far cry from "departure." Even the 1890 Darby Bible—translated by John Nelson Darby, the principal founder of modern-day dispensationalism and largely responsible for popularizing the pre-tribulation rapture—translates this verse with apostasy:

"Let not any one deceive you in any manner, because *it will not be* **unless the apostasy have first come,** and the man of sin have been revealed, the son of perdition."

Is the "falling away" of 2 Thessalonians 2:1-3 the rapture? No. Depending on your perspective of the Greek word *apostasia,* it can either mean a rejection of the faith or a standing away from it. Both cases have negative implications, not one of a rapture or removal of the saints to Heaven prior to the Tribulation. It should be noted that according to this same passage of Scripture, Yeshua will not return until an apostasy takes place and the antimessiah is revealed to the world—and it is actually some of the strongest evidence *against* the pre-tribulation rapture. When put in its proper context, the "falling away" cannot possibly be the rapture. The rejection of/defection from the faith, and the revealing of the antimessiah, must take place first.[31]

"For I am already being poured out as a drink offering, and the time of my departure [*analusis*] has come" (cf. Philippians 1:23).

[31] For a further examination of this issue, consult Chapter 7 of *When Will the Messiah Return?*: "The Great Apostasy." Also consult the relevant sections of the author's commentary *1&2 Thessalonians for the Practical Messianic.*

"I BELIEVE IN THE PRE-TRIBULATION RAPTURE BECAUSE THE JUDGMENTS OF THE TRIBULATION ARE JUST FOR THE JEWS."

Many would view the above statement as being highly anti-Semitic, and they would be correct. The major, contemporary teachers of the pre-tribulation rapture doctrine, are not knowingly anti-Semitic, per se—but a misunderstandings regarding Israel, the Jewish people, and the righteous from the nations do affect their interpretations of Scripture and how they view the Last Days. Many pre-tribulationists *only support* the State of Israel because they believe that Israel's existence as a sovereign country in the Middle East will hasten the pre-tribulation rapture and their escape, not always because they love the Jewish people and have a sincere concern for them and for their knowing Yeshua (Jesus). They would never consider themselves to be a part of the polity of Israel.

Most pre-tribulationists believe that God has two groups of elect: Israel and "the Church," "the Church" being exempt from the Seventieth Week of Israel or Tribulation. However, as post-tribulationists our ministry believes that God has only *one* group of elect, the Commonwealth of Israel (Ephesians 2:11-13) or the Israel of God (Galatians 6:16), in which all Believers are a part—regardless of their ethnicity. (This Israel is also called to follow the Torah or Law of Moses as a part of holy living.)[32]

Some pre-tribulationists have argued, "Jesus was speaking to the Jews in Matthew 24 so that chapter only applies to the Jews." As many non-Jewish post-tribulationists have observed, "If that is truly the case, then I need to dispense with most of Jesus' teachings, because I am not Jewish."[33] The argument which advocates that Yeshua's Olivet Discourse on the Last

---

[32] For a further discussion, consult the author's publication, *Are Non-Jewish Believers Really a Part of Israel?* (forthcoming 2013).

[33] And to this could be added, "Most of the Bible really does not apply to me, either."

Days is only for "the Jews" (Matthew 24; Mark 13; Luke 21) runs into many interpretational problems. The foremost of these problems is that if these words do not apply to today's non-Jewish Believers from the nations, **then what about the rest of the Messiah's teachings?** The vast majority of Yeshua's teachings in the Gospels are directed to a First Century Jewish audience. Do they no longer apply? (Is the ministry of the Messiah largely irrelevant to the vast majority of His followers today?)

The pre-tribulation rapture is based on a misidentification of Israel. It is notable that former Jerusalem chief Rabbi Chaim Richman, present director of the Temple Institute, states, "We [the Jewish people] do not appreciate the idea that the Jews are to be left behind and slaughtered while Christians fly away to heaven."[34] At the very least, the pre-tribulation rapture teaching is a serious deterrent to Jewish evangelism.

Paul warned the non-Jewish Believers in Rome, how those from the nations—the wild olive branches engrafted into Israel's olive tree—that they were not to boast against their Jewish brethren. He writes that if God did not hesitate to cut off some of the natural branches so that wild branches might be grafted into His tree, then He would certainly not hesitate to cut off wild branches. Paul admonishes, "do not be arrogant toward the branches; but if you are arrogant, *remember that* it is not you who supports the root, but the root *supports* you. You will say then, 'Branches were broken off so that I might be grafted in.' Quite right, they were broken off for their unbelief, but you stand by your faith. Do not be conceited, but fear; for if God did not spare the natural branches, He will not spare you, either" (Romans 11:18-21). **How many pre-tribulation rapture Christians take these words seriously enough?** Consider what Paul also says:

"*There will be* tribulation and distress for every soul of man who does evil, of the Jew first and also of the

---

[34] *Orthodox Jews Want the Temple Rebuilt*, Charisma Magazine, June 1993.

Greek, but glory and honor and peace to everyone who does good, to the Jew first and also to the Greek" (Romans 2:9-10).

Both Jewish people and those from the nations are to suffer tribulation together. "God does not show favoritism" (Romans 2:11, NIV).

The issue of the pre-tribulation rapture becomes as much of a question of ecclesiology, or who God's elect is, as it is one of the timing of the Second Coming of Yeshua the Messiah. Pre-tribulationists (and many post-tribulationists for that matter) see "the Church" as an entity separate from Israel. Therefore, pre-tribulationists conclude that "the Church" is removed during the Tribulation period, in reality the Seventieth Week of Israel. If "the Church" and Israel are separate entities, and God has two groups of elect, then the pre-tribulation rapture has more validity. However, *if they are not*, and non-Jewish Believers are incorporated by their faith in Israel's Messiah into an expanded realm of Israel, then the pre-tribulation rapture doctrine—at the very least— deserves some significant reevaluation (if not suffers strong defeat).

Dispensationalists claim that God has temporarily put Israel aside until the Tribulation. It seems that many conveniently forget that without Israel, there would have been no Ten Commandments, no prophesied Messiah, and no salvation. Such are the things that make up an "irrevocable calling" (Romans 11:29). In Ephesians 2:11-13, the Apostle Paul tells us that those who have faith in Yeshua "were estranged from the national life of Isra'el" (Ephesians 2:12, CJB), but now are joined to Israel as "fellow heirs and fellow members" (Ephesians 3:6).

"I BELIEVE IN THE PRE-TRIBULATION RAPTURE BECAUSE THE CHURCH ISN'T MENTIONED AFTER REVELATION 4:1."

In the opening chapters of Revelation (chs. 1-3), the Apostle John was given specific instruction by Yeshua the Messiah, which he was to deliver to the seven assemblies of Asia Minor (Ephesus, Smyrna, Pergamum, Thyatira, Sardis, Philadelphia, Laodicea). After John relayed Yeshua's messages to these congregations, John is told by the Lord, "Come up here, and I will show you what must take place after these things" (Revelation 4:1b). Notice what John said as this command was given to him: "After these things I looked, and behold, a door *standing* open in heaven, and the first voice which I had heard, like *the sound* of a trumpet speaking with me" (Revelation 4:1a). This was a directive that was given only to the Apostle John, as he was called to step into the Heavenly realm, and be shown a vision of the future that, as far as Yeshua and those assembled were concerned, had already taken place. John was asked to step forward in time and be shown things that he did not know about.

This is not a command that is given to "the Church." As Messianics are keen to emphasize, the Greek word *ekklēsia* should be properly translated as either "assembly" or "congregation" in our English Bibles, as opposed to the anachronistic term "church." Likewise, *ekklēsia* was used in the Greek Septuagint to render the Hebrew word *qahal*, referring to the congregation or assembly of Israel, and the Apostolic writers most often use *ekklēsia* with this understanding in mind.[35]

---

[35] *Thayer*, 196 describes how *ekklēsia* "in the Septuagint [is] often equivalent to קָהָל [*qahal*], *the assembly of the Israelites,*" and would have been specifically employed by the Apostles to describe the First Century Body of Messiah's undeniable origins in Ancient Israel.

Cf. K.L. Schmidt, "*ekklēsia*," in Geoffrey W. Bromiley, ed., *Theological Dictionary of the New Testament*, abridged (Grand Rapids: Eerdmans, 1985), pp 397-402.

For a further discussion, consult the author's article "When Did 'the Church' Begin?"

In Johannine literature itself (John, 1-3 John, Revelation) *ekklēsia* **is never used to refer to the Body of Messiah at large, but instead the localized assembly.** Moo poignantly remarks in *Three Views on the Rapture*, "John, himself, never uses ἐκκλησία other than as a designation of a local body of believers. Moreover, it is important to note that John never in chapters 4-19 calls any group in *heaven* the church."[36] The reason that *ekklēsia* does not appear after Revelation 4:1 is because the letters Yeshua had John relay to the seven, localized assemblies of Asia Minor were complete. It is not because "the Church" has been raptured into Heaven. In fact, at the end of Revelation, we are told that the apocalyptic revealing of Yeshua to John is for the *ekklēsia*, strongly implying that the Body of Messiah will be on Earth when these events take place:

"I, Jesus, have sent my angel to testify to you about these things for the churches.[37] I am the root and the descendant of David, the bright morning star" (Revelation 22:16, ESV).

It is notable that there is an urban myth that frequently circulates among Messianic post-tribulationists relating to Revelation 4:1. It often goes along the lines of, "The Church is mentioned after Revelation 4:1—and it is the whore of Babylon!" Unfortunately for those who adhere to this line of reasoning, it is not based in a sound exegesis of the text, nor in a proper evaluation of what end-time Babylon actually is. (It is only based in the insecurities of Messianics who wish to denigrate the positive contributions of the Christian Church.) While there are religious elements of the end-time Babylonian system, there are also political and economic elements. To simply say that end-time Babylon is "the Church," is to misidentify end-time Babylon, which is the multifaceted, anti-God world system.

---

[36] Moo, "The Case for the Posttribulation Rapture Position," in *Three Views on the Rapture*, 201.
[37] Grk. *epi tais ekklēsiais* (ἐπὶ ταῖς ἐκκλησίαις).

"I BELIEVE IN THE PRE-TRIBULATION RAPTURE BECAUSE THE 'DAY OF THE LORD' IS THE RAPTURE."

Many pre-tribulationists, mostly among laypersons, have a mixed view about what the "Day of the LORD" is, because they simply have not done their homework. Many unfortunately believe that the Day of the LORD, or *Yom-ADONAI* (יוֹם־יְהוָה), speaks of their pre-trib escape. The Bible speaks quite profoundly about the Day of the LORD, each reference contingent on context. The Day of the LORD could be in reference to the day of the Messiah coming to judge the world at Armageddon, or it could be in reference to the time period when Yeshua is ruling and reigning from Jerusalem. The Day of the LORD can also be a reference to when God interjects Himself into human lives, enacting help, deliverance, or some other Divine action.[38]

Of a summary of prophecies per the Day of the LORD or *Yom-ADONAI*, we find that a large number of them speak of it being a time of judgment which will then initiate Yeshua's Messianic Kingdom on Earth. Its inevitable arrival is intended to motivate sinners to repentance. Isaiah 13:9-12 tells us,

"Behold, the day of the LORD is coming, cruel, with fury and burning anger, to make the land a desolation; and He will exterminate its sinners from it. For the stars of heaven and their constellations will not flash forth their light; the sun will be dark when it rises and the moon will not shed its light. Thus I will punish the world for its evil and the wicked for their iniquity; I will also put an end to the arrogance of the proud and abase the haughtiness of the ruthless. **I will make mortal man scarcer than pure gold and mankind than the gold of Ophir.**"

The Apostle Peter also says,

---

[38] Cf. "day of the Lord," in Jacob Neusner and William Scott Green, eds., *Dictionary of Judaism in the Biblical Period* (Peabody, MA: Hendrickson, 2002), pp 151-152.

"The Lord is not slow about His promise, as some count slowness, but is patient toward you, not wishing for any to perish but for all to come to repentance. But the day of the Lord will come like a thief, in which the heavens will pass away with a roar and the elements will be destroyed with intense heat, and the earth and its works will be burned up. Since all these things are to be destroyed in this way, what sort of people ought you to be in holy conduct and godliness, looking for and hastening the coming of the day of God, because of which the heavens will be destroyed by burning, and the elements will melt with intense heat! But according to His promise we are looking for new heavens and a new earth, in which righteousness dwells" (2 Peter 3:9-13).

The Day of the LORD and what it composes, will continue to perplex many people who study prophecy until it actually occurs. Clearly, there are aspects of it that are contextual. However, when questioning whether or not "the rapture" is the Day of the LORD, we should compare what happens at the Messiah's Second Coming when He defeats His enemies and rules in power to what the Prophets tell us. On the whole, the Day of the LORD is a time of judgment, not one of levitation up into the clouds.

"I BELIEVE IN THE PRE-TRIBULATION RAPTURE BECAUSE GOD WOULD NOT HAVE ME EXPERIENCE THE TRIBULATION."

This final reason for people believing in the pre-tribulation rapture is by far the most dangerous, because it has to deal directly with the character of God and who He is to an individual person. Many pre-tribulationists when presented with the very fact that they may have to experience general tribulation, *meaning hard times*, may claim that God would never allow it—perhaps suggesting immediately that their god is not the One whom we see depicted in the Holy Scriptures. In fact, some may even go to the extreme by saying that if the pre-tribulation rapture does not occur, then they would deny faith in Messiah Yeshua (Christ Jesus).

In John 17:15, Yeshua prayed, "I do not ask You to take them out of the world, but to keep them from the evil *one*." The Apostle Paul also writes, "Who will separate us from the love of Messiah? Will tribulation, or distress, or persecution, or famine, or nakedness, or peril, or sword?" (Romans 8:35). Are the Scriptures not replete with admonitions for Messiah followers to stand firm in their faith—*ever to the end?*

In His parable of the sower, Yeshua spoke of the one who "has no *firm* root in himself, but is *only* temporary, and when affliction or persecution arises because of the word, immediately he falls away" (Matthew 13:21; cf. Mark 4:17). Many, unfortunately, expect easy, instant answers—when there are none. The hard truth is that those who believe in Yeshua will be persecuted and tribulation does occur. All one has to do is look at a great deal of Church history, and many Believers today who live in the third world, and we see the testimonies of people who have faced extreme circumstances—and in some cases have had to die horrendous deaths for their faith in the Lord.

Some pre-tribulationists I have talked to and corresponded with have even gone as far to say that any microchip implant that could be released on the market for commerce is not the mark of the beast, because the rapture will have not taken place yet.[39] The same put

---

[39] While there is preliminary testing with microchip implants occurring today, we admittedly do not know if these chips will become "the mark," per se. However, we do not encourage **any Believer** to voluntarily receive such an implant. Consult the author's article "What Is the Mark of the Beast?" for a further discussion of this issue.

It is, however, quite disturbing that at least one evangelical Christian voice has completely dismissed this subject, thinking that an implantable microchip for identification might be a good thing Hank Hanegraaf, *The Bible Answer Book 2* (Nashville: Thomas Nelson, 2006), 233 actually said,

"In October 2004 the Food and Drug Administration approved the marketing of a microchip implantable under the skin of humans for medical identification. Paranoid prophecy pundits immediately began touting Verichip technology as the mark of the beast spoken of in Revelation 13. Contrary to such newspaper eschatology, there is no

their eternal destiny on the line for the sake of the non-established pre-tribulation rapture *theory*, which in its modern form is notably *younger* than Charles Darwin's theory of evolution.[40] The pre-tribulation rapture is not *an established fact* **and one would be foolish to put his or her eternal destiny on the line for it.** What if the pre-tribulationist's view of the rapture is incorrect and many so-called "Believers" do take the mark of the beast? Consider Revelation 14:9-11:

"Then another angel, a third one, followed them, saying with a loud voice, 'If anyone worships the beast and his image, and receives a mark on his forehead or on his hand, he also will drink of the wine of the wrath of God, which is mixed in full strength in the cup of His anger; and he will be tormented with fire and brimstone in the presence of the holy angels and in the presence of the Lamb. And the smoke of their torment goes up forever and ever; they have no rest day and night, those who worship the beast and his image, and whoever receives the mark of his name.'"

Revelation 14:9-11 clearly states that those who receive the mark of the beast will be eternally punished. Why would a person put his or her salvation on the line for the sake of a doctrine—and one that is not foundational like the Divinity of Messiah or the inspiration of Holy Scripture? We will probably never know.

Being a pre-tribulationist, post-tribulationist, or holding to any other view does not save you; only having faith in Yeshua the Messiah (Jesus Christ) and being born again does. However, if being a pre-tribulationist dilutes one's thinking to the extent that taking something that may be the mark of the beast is acceptable, then the pre-tribulationist should *seriously* reconsider his or her

---

biblical basis for believing that the mark of the beast is a silicon microchip."

[40] Useful to consider here is the FAQ on the TNN website, "Creationism."

position. It makes one wonder about the spiritual fruit of this belief.

Furthermore, if the pre-tribulationist reading this has a difficult time comprehending the idea that God will allow Believers to experience difficult times, **then think again.** Believers have been persecuted and killed for their faith for centuries—*and our generation is no different.* Let us contemplate the fact that the early Believers in Yeshua, including the Apostles, were under the threat of constant persecution from the Jewish religious authorities, harassment from the Romans, and scores of problems from many pagan locals themselves. But the Lord did not see to it to remove them from those trials. Instead, they endured, and they often used terrible circumstances to testify of their faith (cf. Acts 16:30-32).

What makes us think that we deserve an escape from hard times when they did not get one? *Are we really that presumptuous?* Each one of us who lives in either America or the West needs to go in prayer before God each day and thank Him that we (still) have relative freedom to practice our religious beliefs. One day such freedom is going to be removed, and some are going to be rudely awakened. Some might be really shocked how little faith they actually do have, and others are going to find their faith during an intense time of trial.

-3-

Fifty Evidences
for What?

The reasons we have just provided in the previous chapter are only the common reasons given why pre-tribulationism is supposedly a valid belief. There are, of course, many more reasons that pre-tribulationists will supply. In this chapter, we respond to fifty specific supports given by the late John F. Walvoord (1910-2002) in his book *The Rapture Question*.[1] While we certainly recognize that we could address many more reasons, Walvoord's position as former chancellor of Dallas Theological Seminary, and his vast influence over many other pre-tribulationists, speaks for itself.

We have chosen Walvoord's reasons, as opposed to those of other pre-tribulationists, because of his long-established position as the "dean" of pre-tribulationists. We will assume that because of Walvoord's long-held position in the higher echelons of pre-tribulationism, that his supports for the pre-tribulation rapture represent many, if not most, of those who believe it. These responses by no means should be interpreted as a personal or posthumous attack on Walvoord, but rather a fair post-tribulational criticism of teachings which have influenced millions. There are other, far more serious theological issues that I do share positions in common

---

[1] John F. Walvoord, *The Rapture Question* (Grand Rapids: Zondervan, 1957), pp 191-199.

agreement with Walvoord, and with dispensationalists in general.

(We should make mention of the fact that some of his reasons are used in refutation of mid-tribulationism and partial-rapturism, beliefs we do not hold to. We have nevertheless responded to them to show that while we are in disagreement with Walvoord's pre-tribulational stance, we are *not* in total disagreement with him on other matters.)

Some of our answers to these reasons are going to be very short and others will be more detailed. If they are short, we will be sure to refer you to other writings or articles by our ministry which address the issues more thoroughly. For that same matter, some reasons provided we have already addressed in this analysis and this will be mentioned.

Historical Argument?

1. The early church believed in the imminency of the Lord's return, which is an essential doctrine of pre-tribulationism.

It is very true that the pre-tribulation rapture teaching is very much reliant on the thought that the Messiah's return is "imminent," or the idea that it can occur at any time. However, the Apostle Paul assertively described how before the return of Yeshua there are some events which must take place. He wrote in 2 Thessalonians 2:1-3,

"Now we request you, brethren, with regard to the coming of our Lord Yeshua the Messiah and our gathering together to Him, that you not be quickly shaken from your composure or be disturbed either by a spirit or a message or a letter as if from us, to the effect that the day of the Lord has come. Let no one in any way deceive you, for *it will not come* unless the apostasy comes first, and the man of lawlessness is revealed, the son of destruction."

Paul wrote the Thessalonicans a second time because some had forged letters in his name, or were passing on misinformation, communicating that the end of the world was at hand and the coming of the Messiah was imminent. The apostle assured them that it could not take place until the apostasy or falling away from the faith, and the revealing of the antimessiah/antichrist or man of lawlessness, had occurred. This does not by any means indicate an any-moment, pre-tribulation rapture.

Furthermore, what is considered to be the "early church" here? Is this a statement implying that *all Believers* in the First Century to the Second and Third Centuries believed in some kind of imminence? It is true that segments of Believers in the First Century did believe that the Messiah's return was imminent, and that is why Paul refuted it in his second letter to the Thessalonicans, detailing that certain things had to take place first.

This same kind of anticipation was also evident among various Christian groups of the Second and Third Centuries. But simply because many from the Second and Third Centuries *may* have believed in some kind of imminency, or an any-moment return of the Lord, is not a substantial basis for us to believe it. As post-tribulationist George Eldon Ladd aptly states in his book *The Blessed Hope*, "Let it be at once emphasized that we are not turning to the church fathers to find authority for either pre- or posttribulationism. The one authority is the Word of God, and we are not confined in the straight-jacket of tradition."[2] The history of the emerging Christian Church of the Second and Third Centuries actually shows a wide diversity of views on many theological topics.[3] This is

---

[2] George Eldon Ladd, *The Blessed Hope* (Grand Rapids: Eerdmans, 1956), 19.

[3] In the estimation of Douglas J. Moo, however, "The apostolic Fathers...believed in a posttribulational Rapture *and* expected to participate in tribulation events" ("The Case for the Posttribulation Rapture Position," in *Three Views on the Rapture*, 210), and he offers a selection of ancient references to consider (*Epistle of Barnabas* 4; Justin Martyr *Dialogue with Trypho* 110; *Shepherd of Hermas* 1-3).

most especially true of eschatology up until the more modern period, as Craig S. Keener summarizes in his commentary on Revelation:

"One may take as an example of diverse end-time views among Christians the Millennium, or the thousand-year reign of Christ in Revelation 20. Does Jesus return before the future Millennium (the premillennial view, the most common view among North American evangelicals today) or after it (the postmillennial view), or is this period merely a symbol for the present era (the amillennial view)? Many readers may be surprised to learn that most Christian leaders in history were amillennial (like Augustine, Luther, and Calvin), many leaders in North American revivals were postmillennial (like Jonathan Edwards and Charles Finney), and most of the early church fathers were premillennial (but posttribulational)."[4]

It is important for us to consider the historical record. But, as far as correct doctrine is concerned, our primary source for the truth must first be the authoritative canon of the Holy Bible itself, and not what we might think is the prevailing opinion of those long-since dead, or even the denominational tradition in which we were reared (as beneficial as some of its tenets may be). As Messianic Believers, we certainly know how to break out of "the straight-jacket of tradition," as Ladd puts it. This is not only because a significant number of us are post-tribulationists, but because we are likewise trying to repair some of the damage caused in the Second and Third Centuries, as the Church largely moved away from

---

[4] Craig S. Keener, *NIV Application Commentary: Revelation* (Grand Rapids: Zondervan, 2000), 25.

He goes on to also describe, "If Calvin, Wesley, Finney, Moody, and most Christians today each have held different views, is it possible that God's blessing may not rest solely on those who hold a particular end-time view" (Ibid.) So, even though this publication strongly argues for post-tribulationism, we definitely recognize how pre-tribulationists, and those of other views, have been used mightily by the Lord in ministry and to bring many to a saving knowledge of Himself.

its Hebraic Roots and its social/spiritual ties to the Jewish people.

By the Second and Third Centuries, many in the Church falsely believed that the Torah or Law of Moses was totally abolished by the Messiah,[5] and that the Jewish people were cursed because they "crucified Christ." We know as Messianics that both of these premises are false, because Yeshua plainly states in Matthew 5:17-19 that the Torah stands until Heaven and Earth pass away,[6] and that the Greeks and Romans, pagans, were every bit as responsible for the Messiah's death as the Jewish people—**for all of sinful humanity crucified Christ.**

Nevertheless, we should not simply "accept doctrine" blindly because those of the Second and Third Century Church believed it—or anyone in the past. Nor should we simply accept doctrine because it is the widespread, prevailing, *popular* opinion—or because any "authority" on the subject believes it. The principal reason we should believe a doctrine is because it is a clear teaching of the Word of God and aligns with a correct exegesis of the original Hebrew, Aramaic, and Greek texts. If a doctrine can be supported by history, then that can often be a "bonus," but neither history nor tradition alone should be the principal factors in determining one's theology.

Church history actually demonstrates that the overall prevailing end-time view has been amillennialism, an end-time view developed by Augustine and accepted by the Roman Church, which allegorizes and spiritualizes many end-time judgments and horrors, because the Messiah apparently has the "final victory." If history is the principal determining factor in determining our eschatology, then we really should not be engaged in any

---

[5] This was in full compliance with the Apostle Paul's observation in 2 Thessalonians 2:7, where he stated that in his day "the mystery of lawlessness is already at work." The Complete Jewish Bible appropriately paraphrases this with, "For already this separating from *Torah* is at work secretly."

[6] Consult the author's book *The New Testament Validates Torah* for an exposition of this issue.

kind of pre- versus post-trib rapture debate, because the prophecies of the "end" are largely just allegory. Yet, we should feel that a more literal reading of various prophecies, consistent with the text of Scripture, is something a bit more warranted.

2. The detailed development of pretribulational truth during the past few centuries does not prove that the doctrine is new or novel. Its development is similar to that of other major doctrines in the history of the church.

Whether or not pre-tribulationism was taught in the past and now has been revived over the past two centuries (1800s-present), as some pre-tribulationists may claim, is irrelevant as to whether or not it is Scriptural. It is possible that many in centuries past did believe in pre-tribulationism, or some form of it. But what matters the most is whether or not the Holy Scriptures actually teach it and its ideology of escape prior to the Tribulation can be Biblically justified, which many post-tribulationists do not believe it is.

HERMENEUTICS?

3. Pre-tribulationism is the only view which allows literal interpretation of all Old and New Testament passages on the great tribulation.

We should take this "proof" for pre-tribulationism in light of the times when Walvoord originally wrote his book, *The Rapture Question*, in 1952, only four years after the establishment of the State of Israel in 1948.

Historically, up until very recently, or at least until the establishment of the State of Israel as an independent country, many post-tribulationists have allegorized various end-time prophecies. Or, many post-tribulationists were found to have taken certain liberties with end-time prophecies—liberties with which I do not agree as a post-tribulationist. A strident example of this comes from the fact of some post-tribulationists' interpretation of Matthew 24:22:

"And if those days had not been shortened, no human being would be saved; but for the sake of the elect those days will be shortened" (RSV).

Some post-tribulationists like Robert Gundry[7] interpret this as meaning that the Great Tribulation being three-and-a-half years long is flawed, and that this time will actually be shortened in length. I disagree with post-tribulationists who believe this, and if this is one of the examples being referred to, I would agree that the Scriptural text has probably not been interpreted literally enough by post-tribulationists.

Daniel 12:11 clearly tells us, "From the time that the regular sacrifice is abolished and the abomination of desolation is set up, *there will be* 1,290 days." Some post-tribulationists may tell us that this length of time for the Great Tribulation will be shortened perhaps to 700 or even 500 days, but such a view does challenge the integrity of this prophecy. There is no indication in the text that the number of days will be reduced from 1,290.

The interpretation that I lean to, is that the length of individual days is likely what will be shortened, as a result of the massive Earth changes which are prophesied to take place. For example, Revelation 8:8 says "The second angel sounded, and *something* like a great mountain burning with fire was thrown into the sea; and a third of the sea became blood." Is it possible that as a result of this, and other judgments, that Earth will be thrown off its axis by a meteor or asteroid hitting the planet in such a way that the length of individual days will be reduced from twenty-four hours? I believe that this is a plausible way of how the days will be "shortened," while the number of the days remains the same.

---

[7] Robert H. Gundry, *First the Antichrist* (Grand Rapids: Baker Books, 1997), pp 33-34.

4. Only pre-tribulationism distinguishes clearly between Israel and the church and their respective programs.

Here, the pre-tribulationists are absolutely correct. Pre-tribulationism is the only end-time view which clearly maintains a (rigid) distinction between Israel and "the Church." Post-tribulationists have a very difficult time placing both groups into the Seventieth Week of Israel, without problems, or resorting to replacement theology.

Many of today's Messianic Jewish Believers, and Messianic non-Jewish Believers, accept the widespread view that God has two groups of elect: Israel and "the Church." Many others in today's Messianic community, however, believe that God has only one chosen assembly: the Commonwealth of Israel *of which all Believers are a part*. The Apostle Paul wrote non-Jewish Believers in Asia Minor that before they came to faith in Yeshua, they were "excluded from citizenship in Israel and foreigners to the covenants of the promise, without hope and without God in the world" (Ephesians 2:12, NIV). But now that these people had come to faith, they were now considered a part of the Commonwealth of Israel, as "fellow heirs and fellow members of the body, and fellow partakers of the promise in Messiah Yeshua through the gospel" (Ephesians 3:6). They were not considered part of a separate "Church," but were instead part of the Israel of God (Galatians 6:16), grafted-in to Israel's olive tree by faith in Israel's Messiah (Romans 11:16-17).

As far as pre-tribulationism is concerned, its adherents are entirely right in that pre-tribulationism is the only end-time view that clearly distinguishes separate programs for Israel and "the Church." But since we reject the false belief of "separate programs," as it is commonly termed, we do not accept pre-tribulationism.

NATURE OF THE
TRIBULATION?

5. Pre-tribulationism maintains Scriptural distinction between the great tribulation and the tribulation in general which precedes it.

In John 16:33, Messiah Yeshua says, "These things I have spoken to you, so that in Me you may have peace. In the world you have tribulation, but take courage; I have overcome the world." The Greek word translated "tribulation" in this passage is *thlipsis* (θλῖψις), meaning, **"trouble that inflicts distress, *oppression, affliction, tribulation*"** (*BDAG*).[8] *Thlipsis* is the same term used in critical end-time passages such as: Matthew 24:9, 21, 29; Mark 13:19, 24; and Revelation 7:14.

Many Pre-tribulationists try to tell us that there is a "distinct difference" between what we might call "simple" or "generic" tribulation, or hard times and oppression, and the prophesied Great Tribulation or *thlipsis megalē* (θλῖψις μεγάλη), meaning the latter half of Daniel's Seventieth Week that Yeshua refers to: "For then there will be a great tribulation, such as has not occurred since the beginning of the world until now, nor ever will" (Matthew 24:21).

The Apostle Paul writes the Romans, "*There will be tribulation and distress for every soul of man who does evil, of the Jew first and also of the Greek...And not only this, but we also exult in our tribulations, knowing that tribulation brings about perseverance...Who will separate us from the love of Messiah? Will tribulation, or distress, or persecution, or famine, or nakedness, or peril, or sword?*" (Romans 2:9, 5:3; 8:35). Paul also writes them, "*Be devoted to one another in brotherly love; give preference to one another in honor; not lagging behind in diligence, fervent in spirit, serving the Lord; rejoicing in*

---

[8] *BDAG*, 457.

hope, **persevering in tribulation**, devoted to prayer" (Romans 12:10-12).

Paul says that Believers are to "be patient in tribulation" (RSV). The Greek verb *hupomenō* (ὑπομένω) is defined by *BDAG* as "**to maintain a belief or course of action in the face of opposition**, *stand one's ground, hold out, endure.*"[9] Regardless of the circumstances, whether Believers find themselves in "general" tribulation or the Great Tribulation, they are called to hold fast to their faith in Messiah Yeshua. While there is a textual distinction to be found between "tribulation" and the "Great Tribulation" in Scripture, if we are true Believers and we find ourselves in the Great Tribulation, we are called to hold fast to our faith. However, as it pertains to the issues at hand, it must and should be noted that some pre-tribulationists are extremely manipulative when it comes to "tribulation," *regardless* of how it is used. Consider the following words of popular author Tim LaHaye in the opening pages of his 1998 book *Rapture Under Attack*:[10]

> "Prisoners have looked expectantly through dungeon windows. Slaves have looked up from the fields. Children have wondered at a slant of sunlight through a sudden break in the clouds. Jesus is coming. Soon! Maybe today. Maybe tonight. Maybe before I draw my next breath.
>
> "And yet that comforting belief is under greater attack today more than at any time in recent history. Christian mothers now worry that their precious sons and daughters will be forced to undergo the horrors of the Great Tribulation. Christian fathers fret about the impossible task of keeping their families alive through the most gruesome period the world has ever known."[11]

---

[9] Ibid., 1039.

[10] Note that *Rapture Under Attack*, printed in 1998, was originally released under the title of *No Fear of the Storm* in 1992, and then re-released in 2002 as *The Rapture*.

[11] Tim LaHaye, *Rapture Under Attack* (Sisters, OR: Multomah Publishing, 1998), pp 19-20.

Hopefully, you can see the escapist ideology omanating from these manipulative words. They speak of the fear that pre-tribulationists have, most notably among many American Christians, of perhaps facing the horrors of the end-times. *Whatever happened to born again Believers placing **their complete trust and confidence** in a Sovereign, Creator God?*

Without any doubt, none of us should ever want to face the antimessiah/antichrist or experience the Tribulation period. But if we are steadfast in the faith, and we have some assurance of our salvation, then we should be willing to die for the cause of the Messiah—something seldom, if ever, emphasized among that many American Christians today. Yeshua said in Acts 1:8, "you shall be My witnesses both in Jerusalem, and in all Judea and Samaria, and even to the remotest part of the earth." Looking back on this many centuries forward, we do find that *martus* (μάρτυς), "witness," is the root word for *martyr*. We are called—if indeed necessary—to be martyrs for the faith.

This is something that is simply unpopular among many of the "Christian Believers" of today, who in various degrees are (seriously) compromised with the world. *Hearing about the possibility of dying for the faith certainly does not sell books.* LaHaye's words continue, as he says, "Are you able to impress on your teenagers the need to live pure lives in the constant expectation of the Lord's sudden return?"[12] Perhaps the better question would be: "How do we live set-apart and holy lives so not to compromise ourselves with the world and live in sin?" How do we endure whatever life circumstances we may face, which may have to prepare us for more difficult circumstances of the long term future?

In response to this and other similar claims, I wrote the following in my book *When Will the Messiah Return?*:

---

[12] Ibid., 20.

Although many pre-tribulationists will claim that their view stimulates an urgency to spread the gospel message, as the Messiah can supposedly return at any moment, the actions of many individual pre-tribulationists do not always reflect this intent. It has been my personal experience that many people who endorse a pre-tribulation rapture are not that eager to spread the good news, and would just assume to "live it up now" as the Lord can supposedly return in the next hour, minute, or even second. I concede that this view may only be held by some (who would likely never admit it), but the Bible is quite clear that certain events must precede the return of the Messiah. Yeshua the Messiah **cannot return at "any moment."** God's people are to have the utmost wisdom, discernment, and productivity in the time which leads up to the Messiah's return.

Many of the same pre-tribulationists who say that pre-tribulationism stimulates an urgency to spread the gospel, may say that post-tribulationism does not stimulate such an urgency and encourages spiritual laxness. I would have to consider this impossible, especially as we consider the fact that if Believers are to go through the Tribulation period, some may have to be horrifically martyred for the faith. **This certainly does not sound like spiritual laxness!** The unpopular reality of possibly being martyred is not something that most pre-tribulationists readily think about, emphasize, or even discuss in their teachings.[13]

My comments are likewise mirrored by post-tribulationist William Arnold, who writes in his booklet *The Post-Tribulation Rapture,*

"The argument is that pre-tribulationism keeps everybody 'on their toes,' whereas post-tribulationism leads towards a lukewarm lifestyle. Well, I am a post-tribulationist and as I consider that I may one day suffer persecution and possibly even give my life for my faith in Christ, 'lukewarm' is hardly the attitude which comes to mind...I could just as easily argue that because of pre-tribulationism many people figure that they'll just wait

---

[13] J.K. McKee, *When Will the Messiah Return?* (Kissimmee, FL: TNN Press, 2012 printing), 37.

and see what happens, and, if they miss the first boat, they'll just catch the second one. I think that Jesus warned us of the Tribulation so that we would prepare to endure this difficult time."[14]

While there are contextual distinctions between "tribulation," in reference to difficult times, and then the "Great Tribulation," or the last half of the Seventieth Week of Israel—pre-tribulationists often do a great disservice in not examining the fact that the Scriptures admonish Messiah followers to persevere through tribulation or terrible distress. **Tribulation is to enable us to rely more on God, not less on Him.**

In our day, particularly as the Messianic movement grows, many non-Jewish Believers are seeing the errors of pre-tribulationism, and are recognizing themselves as a part of Israel. The Hebrew name *Yisrael* (יִשְׂרָאֵל) means "God prevails." J.H. Hertz tells us in his commentary *Pentateuch & Haftorahs* that "The name is clearly a title of victory; probably 'a champion of God'. The children of the Patriarch are *Israelites*, Champions of God, Contenders for the Divine, conquering by strength from Above."[15] These people are striving to see their relationship with the Lord reinvigorated—reading not only the Apostolic Scriptures (New Testament), but also the Tanach (Old Testament)—and notably seeing how His people *have always prevailed* through hardships.

The name Israel does not mean "one who escapes with God," but instead communicates how God's people are called to prevail with Him. We are not called to seek escapist ends. We are called to endure because it indicates how much faith we truly have in God, and whether or not we believe that He is powerful to deliver us through difficult times.

---

[14] William Arnold, *The Post-Tribulation Rapture* (Stockton, CA: Author, 1999), 50.

[15] J.H. Hertz, ed., *Pentateuch & Haftorahs* (London: Soncino Press, 1960), 124.

6. The great tribulation is properly interpreted by pretribulationists as a time of preparation for Israel's restoration (Deut. 4:29-30; Jer. 30:4-11). It is not the purpose of the tribulation to prepare the church for glory.

Pre-tribulationists asserting that the Tribulation period, or the Seventieth Week of Israel, is a time for the "preparation for Israel's restoration," are indeed correct. Of course, the obvious problem that we run into here is that they believe that God has two groups of elect, Israel and "the Church," which we do not accept to be true. Concluding that all Messiah followers are a part of the Commonwealth of Israel (Ephesians 2:11-13) or the Israel of God (Galatians 6:16), with non-Jewish grafted-in to Israel's olive tree (Romans 11:16-17), the restoration of Israel's Kingdom is indeed something we should all look forward to—and it is not something that concerns the Jewish people exclusively. Israel's restoration is something, after all, that does affect the *entire world*. James the Just predicated the salvation of the nations in the First Century, on the basis that they would be a part of an enlarged realm of Israel (Acts 15:15-18; Amos 9:11-12).

The verses referenced by Walvoord are very correct in that they speak of the restoration of the Kingdom to Israel:

"But from there you will seek the LORD your God, and you will find *Him* if you search for Him with all your heart and all your soul. When you are in distress and all these things have come upon you, in the latter days you will return to the LORD your God and listen to His voice" (Deuteronomy 4:29-30).

The Torah tells us that in the Last Days when the people of Israel, who have been scattered into the nations of the world, turn in repentance toward the Lord, that they will return to the Land of Israel. The Hebrew word translated "distress" is *tzar* (צַר) and its equivalent word in the Greek Septuagint is *thlipsis* (θλῖψις), the same commonly translated "tribulation." Hertz offers some valuable commentary when he says, "it was in the Exile that repentant Israel found God, rediscovered the Torah, rediscovered itself."[16] We have seen many Jewish people come to faith in Messiah Yeshua over the past fifty years. And, in our day many Christians who have known Yeshua as their Lord and Savior are rediscovering and following the Torah. They are all recognizing themselves as a part of Israel with a Divine mission to fulfill. Does it indicate that these prophecies are in the midst of occurring? Consider the second passage Walvoord references:

> "Now these are the words which the LORD spoke concerning Israel and concerning Judah: For thus says the LORD, 'I have heard a sound of terror, of dread, and there is no peace. Ask now, and see if a male can give birth. Why do I see every man *with* his hands on his loins, as a woman in childbirth? And *why* have all faces turned pale? Alas! for that day is great, there is none like it; and it is the time of Jacob's distress, but he will be saved from it. It shall come about on that day,' declares the LORD of hosts, 'that I will break his yoke from off their neck and will tear off their bonds; and strangers will no longer make them their slaves. But they shall serve the LORD their God and David their king, whom I will raise up for them. Fear not, O Jacob My servant,' declares the LORD, 'And do not be dismayed, O Israel; for behold, I will save you from afar and your offspring from the land of their captivity. And Jacob will return and will be quiet and at ease, and no one will make him afraid. For I am with you,' declares the LORD, 'to save you; for I will destroy completely all the nations where I have scattered you, only I will not destroy you completely. But I will chasten you justly and will by no means leave you unpunished'" (Jeremiah 30:4-11).

This second set of verses indeed speaks of the Last Days, the judgment, and then the restoration of Israel and Judah. These verses speak of a "time of trouble for Jacob" (NJPS).[17] But note that God also says, "I am with you and

---

[16] Hertz, 762.

[17] Heb. *et-tzarah hee l'Ya'akov* (עֵת־צָרָה הִיא לְיַעֲקֹב).

will save you...Though I completely destroy all the nations among which I scatter you, I will not completely destroy you" (NIV). The most important point emphasized appears in v. 10, where the Lord says, "Fear not, O Jacob My servant...And do not be dismayed, O Israel; for behold, I will save you from afar and your offspring from the land of their captivity. And Jacob will return and will be quiet and at ease, and no one will make him afraid."

These are some very powerful statements made. They clearly attest to the fact that God will "save" His people. The verb *yasha* (יָשַׁע), appearing in the Hifil stem (casual action, active voice), means "to **help, save** (from danger)" and "to **come to assist with**" (*HALOT*).[18] Not surprisingly, it comes from the root for our Messiah's Hebrew name *Yeshua* (יֵשׁוּעַ). The Lord tells us that Israel will return to the Promised Land and "no one will make him afraid." While non-Jewish Believers should not expect to participate in a return to the Promised Land, and take up some kind of tribal inheritance, they are nonetheless a part of Israel's polity. For, tribulation is equally for the Jew and Greek together (Romans 2:9).

Before Yeshua's ascension into Heaven, Acts 1:6-7 tells us, "when they had come together, they were asking Him, saying, 'Lord, is it at this time You are restoring the kingdom to Israel?' He said to them, 'It is not for you to know times or epochs which the Father has fixed by His own authority.'" Yeshua's Disciples inquired about when the Kingdom was going to be restored to Israel. This restoration is something that still has not occurred, but it will be the end result of Daniel's Seventieth Week. Daniel 9:24 says, "Seventy weeks have been decreed for your people and your holy city, to finish the transgression, to make an end of sin, to make atonement for iniquity, to bring in everlasting righteousness, to seal up vision and prophecy and to anoint the most holy *place*."

---

[18] Ludwig Koehler and Walter Baumgartner, eds., *The Hebrew & Aramaic Lexicon of the Old Testament*, 2 vols. (Leiden, the Netherlands: Brill, 2001), 1:448-449.

These are the goals which all of us should endeavor to see fulfilled one day. Make no mistake about it: the Kingdom of God is the Kingdom realm of Israel. Every Believer in Israel's Messiah has a stake in what is to take place in the future.

7. None of the Old Testament passages on the tribulation mention the church (Deut. 4:29-30; Jer. 30:4-11; Dan. 9:24-27; 12:1-2).

Because our ministry believes that God does not have two groups of elect, Israel and "the Church"—and instead that all Believers are a part of the polity of Israel—we accept the statement that these Tanach or Old Testament passages do not speak of a second group of elect, which we do not believe exists. Israel experiences the Tribulation, and with all Messiah followers being a part of Israel, we should expect to experience it. *Hopefully, we believe that the Lord is powerful enough to deliver us through it.*

We just examined Deuteronomy 4:29-30 and Jeremiah 30:4-11 previously in #6. We now examine the other referenced passages, beginning with Daniel 9:24-27:

> "Seventy weeks have been decreed for your people and your holy city, to finish the transgression, to make an end of sin, to make atonement for iniquity, to bring in everlasting righteousness, to seal up vision and prophecy and to anoint the most holy *place.* So you are to know and discern *that* from the issuing of a decree to restore and rebuild Jerusalem until Messiah the Prince *there will be* seven weeks and sixty-two weeks; it will be built again, with plaza and moat, even in times of distress. Then after the sixty-two weeks the Messiah will be cut off and have nothing, and the people of the prince who is to come will destroy the city and the sanctuary. And its end *will come* with a flood; even to the end there will be war; desolations are determined. And he will make a firm covenant with the many for one week, but in the middle of the week he will put a stop to sacrifice and grain offering; and on the wing of

abominations *will come* one who makes desolate, even until a complete destruction, one that is decreed, is poured out on the one who makes desolate."

Daniel 9:24-27 does speak of the Tribulation period relating to Israel. Obviously, there are expectations regarding the restoration of Israel in the end-times, which specifically concern physical descendants of the Patriarchs Abraham, Isaac, and Jacob. Non-Jewish Believers who are a part of Israel's polity, though, are still going to experience the difficulties leading up to the Second Coming, along with their fellow Jewish brothers and sisters.

The Seventy Weeks prophecy, when completed, will result in the full restoration of Israel's Kingdom in the subsequent Millennium. Ironically, perhaps, many dispensationalists believe that Christians (even those returned from Heaven after the pre-tribulation rapture) will be a part of this Millennial Kingdom, involving a restored twelve tribes of Israel in the Holy Land, and an expanded realm of Israel encompassing all nations (Amos 9:11-12).

The last passage referenced is Daniel 12:1-2:

> "Now at that time Michael, the great prince who stands *guard* over the sons of your people, will arise. And there will be a time of distress such as never occurred since there was a nation until that time; and at that time your people, everyone who is found written in the book, will be rescued. Many of those who sleep in the dust of the ground will awake, these to everlasting life, but the others to disgrace *and* everlasting contempt."

Daniel 12:1-2 is again a reference to Israel. As previously stated, we believe that the Archangel Michael, the great prince, is the restrainer mentioned in 2 Thessalonians 2:6-7. By no means is Michael the great prince or *ha'sar ha'gadol* (הַשַּׂר הַגָּדוֹל) of "the Church"—because "the Church" as a second group of elect does not exist. Lest we draw the conclusion that "your people" in Daniel 12:1-2 only involves the Jewish people, James the Just attested in Acts 15:14, "Simeon has related how God first concerned Himself about taking from among the Gentiles a people for His name." It is widely agreed among interpreters that James' word is rooted within the sentiment of Zechariah 2:11, "Many nations will join themselves to the LORD in that day and will become My people. Then I will dwell in your midst, and you will know that the LORD of hosts has sent Me to you." It is fair to assert that Michael guarding the people of God, involves both the Jewish people and those from the nations who recognize Israel's God.

8. None of the New Testament passages on the tribulation mention the church (Matt. 24:15-31; 1 Thess. 1:9-10, 5:4-9; Rev. 4-19).

This statement is accurate, because the references provided as a support for pre-tribulationism do not mention "the Church," but instead, either directly or inferred, refer to Israel. Once again, because we do not accept the widely held belief that God has two groups of elect, and instead are of the position that all Believers are a part of an enlarged polity of Israel, when Israel is referred to in these passages it does include non-Jewish Believers in Israel's Messiah, and not exclusively ethnic Jews and/or Messianic Jewish Believers saved during the Tribulation period, as pre-tribulationists often advocate.

We will now examine the various passages referenced, beginning with Yeshua's words in His Olivet Discourse:

> "Therefore when you see the ABOMINATION OF DESOLATION [Daniel 9:27] which was spoken of through Daniel the prophet, standing in the holy place (let the reader understand), then those who are in Judea must flee to the mountains. Whoever is on the housetop must not go down to get the things out that are in his house. Whoever is in the field must not turn back to get his cloak. But woe to those who are pregnant and to those who are nursing babies in those days! But pray that your flight will not be in the winter, or on a Sabbath. For then there will be a great tribulation, such as has

not occurred since the beginning of the world until
now, nor ever will. Unless those days had been cut
short, no life would have been saved; but for the sake of
the elect those days will be cut short. Then if anyone
says to you, 'Behold, here is the Messiah,' or 'There *He
is*,' do not believe *him*. For false Messiahs and false
prophets will arise and will show great signs and
wonders, so as to mislead, if possible, even the elect.
Behold, I have told you in advance. So if they say to
you, 'Behold, He is in the wilderness,' do not go out, *or*,
'Behold, He is in the inner rooms,' do not believe *them*.
For just as the lightning comes from the east and flashes
even to the west, so will the coming of the Son of Man
be. Wherever the corpse is, there the vultures will
gather. But immediately after the tribulation of those
days THE SUN WILL BE DARKENED, AND THE MOON WILL
NOT GIVE ITS LIGHT, AND THE STARS WILL FALL from the
sky, and the powers of the heavens will be shaken. And
then the sign of the Son of Man will appear in the sky,
and then all the tribes of the earth will mourn, and they
will see the SON OF MAN COMING ON THE CLOUDS OF THE
SKY with power and great glory. And He will send forth
His angels with A GREAT TRUMPET and THEY WILL
GATHER TOGETHER His elect from the four winds, from
one end of the sky to the other[19]" (Matthew 24:15-31).

Matthew 24:15-31 does not mention "the Church,"
which is believed to be a group of chosen ones separate
from the community of Israel. From the pre-
tribulationist's perspective, these verses do not concern
them because as part of "the Church" they will be
raptured to Heaven prior to the Tribulation period, and
Jesus was only speaking to the Jews anyway.[20] Alas, what
cannot go unnoticed is that passages like Matthew 24:15-

---

[19] Cf. Isaiah 13:10; Ezekiel 32:7; Joel 2:10, 31; 3:15.

[20] Indeed, it must be emphasized once again, if post-tribulational
passages like Matthew 24:29-31 can be pawned off as not applying to
"the Church," with the reason that "Jesus was only speaking to Jews,"
how much more of the Gospels—or even the Bible—does not apply to
non-Jewish Believers based on the same reasoning? This
dispensationalist hermeneutic has caused considerable damage to the
Body of Messiah, sometimes neutering Believers from focusing on the
wider message of the Biblical text, most especially the Tanach or Old
Testament.

31 compose "the word of the Lord" (1 Thessalonians 4:15ff.), and would be some of the few explicit teachings from the Messiah Himself about His return and the anticipated resurrection of the dead.[21]

If you have carefully reviewed Matthew 24:15-31, you can see some obvious problems with a pre-tribulational point of view, such as the fact that Yeshua returns to gather the elect "after the tribulation." But even more importantly, if these verses do not concern members of "the Church," and should be largely ignored as not really applying to Believers, then it should not be surprising why various Christians today could be said to be falling into the various traps warned against. Take important note of the following warnings Yeshua the Messiah gives, which we should supposedly disregard in some way because they do not apply to "the Church":

"For false messiahs and false prophets will appear and produce great signs and omens, to lead astray, if possible, even the elect. Take note, I have told you beforehand" (Matthew 24:24-25, NRSV).

The warning against false messiahs, false prophets, and also false teachers, is evident throughout the Scriptures. There will be those in the Last Days who will claim to be followers of Yeshua the Messiah (Jesus Christ), when in actuality they are not. They will show false signs and false miracles and bring in false teachings that will deceive many. The Apostle Paul wrote Timothy that "the time will come when they will not endure sound doctrine; but *wanting* to have their ears tickled, they will accumulate for themselves teachers in accordance to their own desires" (2 Timothy 4:3). He also wrote him, "the Spirit explicitly says that in later times some will fall away from the faith, paying attention to deceitful spirits and doctrines of demons, by means of the hypocrisy of liars seared in their own conscience as with a branding iron" (1 Timothy 4:1-2).

---

[21] For a further discussion, consult the relevant sections of the author's commentary *1&2 Thessalonians for the Practical Messianic*.

Is one of the specific false teachings that will be disseminated in the Last Days, actually the pre-tribulation rapture? Consider what Yeshua specifically warns will be said by those who will be demonstrating the false signs and wonders:

"Then if anyone says to you, 'Look, here is the Christ!' or 'There he is!' do not believe it" (Matthew 24:23, ESV).

Specifically, these false messiahs or false "anointed ones," false prophets, and false teachers, will say, "Look! He's hidden away in a secret room!" (Matthew 24:26, CJB). *Could this be a direct reference in Scripture to pre-tribulationism?* Do pre-tribulationists not tell us that Yeshua is going to come and take us to the "secret inner chambers," away from the difficult times of the Tribulation? It really might not be that surprising why teachers of pre-tribulationism want Matthew 24 to only apply to Israel and not to them—because it may be that Yeshua's warning speaks of them! It is certainly a reference to escapist teachings.

Another phenomenon of the end-times is mentioned by the Apostle Peter, who astutely warns,

"But false prophets also arose among the people, just as there will also be false teachers among you, who will secretly introduce destructive heresies, even denying the Master who bought them, bringing swift destruction upon themselves. Many will follow their sensuality, and because of them the way of the truth will be maligned" (2 Peter 2:1-2).

The Greek term translated as "sensuality" or "licentiousness" (RSV) is *aselgeia* (ἀσέλγεια). It specifically means "**lack of self-restraint which involves one in conduct that violates all bounds of what is socially acceptable,** *self-abandonment*" (*BDAG*).[22] Jude employs this same term in his epistle, perhaps reflecting on Peter's warning, where he writes, "For certain persons have crept in unnoticed, those who were long beforehand marked

---

[22] *BDAG*, 141.

out for this condemnation, ungodly persons who turn the grace of our God into licentiousness [*aselgeia*] and deny our only Master and Lord, Yeshua the Messiah" (Jude 4).

How can teachers turn the grace of God into licentiousness—total debauchery? They falsely assert that Yeshua the Messiah came to completely abolish the Torah or the Law of Moses, rather than uphold it and show His followers how to live it properly. Not surprisingly, many of those who preach pre-tribulationism proclaim this, saying that God's Torah is only for the Jews, and that it is largely irrelevant for Christians (aside for being a part of Biblical history). Many of those who are pre-tribulationists do not uphold the continued authority of the Tanach or Old Testament or even the Ten Commandments for Believers today as valid moral or ethical instruction. Yeshua likewise warns us of this in the Olivet Discourse when He says, "Because lawlessness will multiply, the love of many will grow cold" (Matthew 24:12, HCSB).

The next set of verses referenced by Walvoord are 1 Thessalonians 1:9-10 and 5:4-9:

> "For they themselves report about us what kind of a reception we had with you, and how you turned to God from idols to serve a living and true God, and to wait for His Son from heaven, whom He raised from the dead, *that is* Yeshua, who rescues us from the wrath to come" (1 Thessalonians 1:9-10).

> "But you, brethren, are not in darkness, that the day would overtake you like a thief; for you are all sons of light and sons of day. We are not of night nor of darkness; so then let us not sleep as others do, but let us be alert and sober. For those who sleep do their sleeping at night, and those who get drunk get drunk at night. But since we are of *the* day, let us be sober, having put on the breastplate of faith and love, and as a helmet, the hope of salvation. For God has not destined us for wrath, but for obtaining salvation through our Lord Yeshua the Messiah" (1 Thessalonians 5:4-9).

These passages are supposed to speak of "the Church" being spared from the Tribulation period, i.e., "the wrath to come." The Greek term for "wrath" here is *orgē* (ὀργή), which as we have discussed previously is used in the Book of Revelation in a post-tribulational context, and does not apply to the entire Seventieth Week of Israel (Revelation 6:16-17; 11:18; 16:19). This *orgē* or Divine wrath also refers to those who experience eternal punishment in the Lake of Fire (Revelation 14:10), something that Messiah Yeshua has certainly delivered Believers from! The admonition of 1 Thessalonians 5:4-9 is that Believers are to be on guard and sober, vigilant in their faith—not seeking an any-moment escape. There are too many (claiming) Believers who are spiritual drunkards and in a stupor, believing that the Messiah will return at any moment—for whom He sadly may catch off guard as a thief *or burglar!*

The last reference offered by Walvoord is Revelation chs. 4-19. We have already addressed this to an extent, stating that the Apostle John in his writings only uses *ekklēsia* or "assembly" (most often poorly rendered as "church") to refer to individual assemblies or congregations, and not the corporate Body of Messiah. Nevertheless, pre-tribulationists do want us to believe that since *ekklēsia* is not used in Revelation chs. 4-19 that "the Church" has been raptured to Heaven. Yet, it is only the Apostle John who is told to come up into Heaven by Yeshua, and not the *ekklēsia:*

> "After these things I [John] looked, and behold, a door *standing* open in heaven, and the first voice which I had heard, like *the sound* of a trumpet speaking with me, said, 'Come up here, and I will show you what must take place after these things'" (Revelation 4:1).

9. In contrast to midtribulationism, the pretribulational view provides an adequate explanation for the beginning of the great tribulation in Revelation 6. Midtribulationism is refuted by the plain teaching of Scripture that the great tribulation begins long before the seventh trumpet of Revelation 11.

This is a pre-tribulational argument against mid-tribulationism, a teaching which advocates that Believers are removed from Planet Earth at the middle of the Seventieth Week of Israel. We are post-tribulationists and as such do not advocate mid-tribulationism. We consider mid-tribulationism to be a "middle position" compromise between pre- and post-tribulationism. In this case, our disagreement with the mid-tribulationists is that we hold that Believers are on Planet Earth during the Great Tribulation, and our disagreement with pre-tribulationists is that we hold that Believers are not spared from the first three-and-a-half years, either.

10. The proper distinction is maintained between the prophetic trumpets of Scripture by pretribulationism. There is no proper ground for the pivotal argument of midtribulationism that the seventh trumpet of Revelation is the last trumpet in that there is no established connection between the seventh trumpet of Revelation 11, the last trumpet of 1 Corinthians 15:52, and the trumpet of Matthew 24:31. They are three distinct events.

This is another pre-tribulational claim against mid-tribulationism, and we emphasize once again that we are not mid-tribulationists. However, since mid-tribulationism does attach a significant importance to the "last trumpet" here, pre-tribulationists assume that there are differences between the trumpets of Matthew 24:31, 1 Corinthians 15:52, and the seventh trumpet of Revelation 11. Walvoord just states his view of how "there is no established connection...They are three distinct events."

However, what should immediately be obvious to the critical reader is that no reason or Scriptural support is given as to *why* these must, or even should, be considered three distinct and separate events. I point this out because as a post-tribulationist, I hold that they are one and the same event. These verses are quoted below, first with Yeshua's words in Matthew, followed by His Revelation to John, and then with Paul's admonition to the Corinthians:

> "But immediately after the tribulation of those days THE SUN WILL BE DARKENED, AND THE MOON WILL NOT GIVE ITS LIGHT, AND THE STARS WILL FALL from the sky, and the powers of the heavens will be shaken. And then the sign of the Son of Man will appear in the sky, and then all the tribes of the earth will mourn, and they will see the SON OF MAN COMING ON THE CLOUDS OF THE SKY with power and great glory. And He will send forth His angels with A GREAT TRUMPET and THEY WILL GATHER TOGETHER His elect from the four winds, from one end of the sky to the other" (Matthew 24:29-31).[23]

> "Then the seventh angel sounded; and there were loud voices in heaven, saying, 'The kingdom of the world has become *the kingdom* of our Lord and of His Messiah; and He will reign forever and ever'" (Revelation 11:15).

> "Behold, I tell you a mystery; we will not all sleep, but we will all be changed, in a moment, in the twinkling of an eye, at the last trumpet; for the trumpet will sound, and the dead will be raised imperishable, and we will be changed" (1 Corinthians 15:51-52).

The Messiah plainly stated that He will gather the saints "after the tribulation of those days...with a loud trumpet call" (ESV); at the seventh trumpet the kingdom of the world becomes that of Yeshua; and at the last trumpet the resurrection and transformation of the saints occurs. Why can we not view these three verses as speaking of the same event? Is it somehow because the idea of going through the Tribulation period is

---

[23] Cf. Isaiah 13:10; Ezekiel 32:7; Joel 2:10, 31; 3:15.

unpopular? We may never know the pre-tribulationist's reasoning that suggests these are three separate events, rather than these being three descriptions of the *same event.*

11. The unity of Daniel's seventieth week is maintained by pretribulationists. By contrast, midtribulationism destroys the unity of Daniel's seventieth week and confuses Israel's program with that of the church.

As Messianics who believe that all those who have faith in Messiah Yeshua are a part of the Commonwealth of Israel—a mixed assembly of Jewish and non-Jewish Believers—we do not recognize "the Church" as a second group of elect outside of Israel. We consider "the Church," as defined by dispensationalism as a separate group of elect, to largely be a man-made institution and category.[24] As we get closer and closer to the return of the Messiah, and continue to witness the growth and expansion of the contemporary Messianic movement— non-Jewish Believers who join in unity with their fellow Jewish Believers will see themselves, more and more, as a part of Israel's Kingdom realm.

Our Heavenly Father has only one group of elect, and a straightforward reading of Yeshua's prayer of John 17 would not at all support an ideal of the Lord possessing two groups of elect.

---

[24] I would note for you that many of the theologians I engage with in the *Practical Messianic* commentary series, who use the term "church," do so principally to speak of a localized assembly. While at times it is necessary to clarify a quotation or two with an explanatory remark in brackets [], I do not frequently do this when a localized congregation is being referred to.

NATURE OF THE CHURCH?

12. The translation of the church is never mentioned in any passage dealing with the Second Coming of Christ after the tribulation.

We do not need to answer this claim again, considering that "the Church" does not exist as a second group of elect. Truly, Walvoord and company *would recognize* that Israel is present in the Second Coming passages, and since we believe that the *qahal/ekklēsia* of God is a Kingdom realm of Israel composed of Jewish and non-Jewish Messiah followers, Believers are present at His Second Coming after the Tribulation.

13. The church is not appointed to wrath (Romans 5:9; 1 Thes. 5:1-9). The church therefore cannot enter "the great day of their wrath" (Rev. 6:17).

We will address each of these verses one at a time. Please keep in mind, however, that we have already discussed how Believers are spared from the *orgē* (ὀργή) of God, this "wrath" being the judgment primarily relating to the eternal punishment of the Lake of Fire—which all those who have salvation are certainly spared from. The first reference offered says,

"Much more then, having now been justified by His blood, we shall be saved from the wrath [*orgē*] of God through Him" (Romans 5:9).

Romans 5:9 is used as proof to speak of "the Church" not entering into the wrath of God. We certainly affirm that Believers will not be subjected to His *orgē*, but it is interesting that the term *ekklēsia* is not used in this verse, nor in Romans ch. 5 at all. Interestingly enough, the Apostle Paul writes previously in Romans 5:1-4 that Messiah followers are to *endure tribulation*, not only not alluding to any pre-tribulation rapture escape, but for that matter any kind of complete escape from terrible circumstances in life:

"Therefore, having been justified by faith, we have peace with God through our Lord Yeshua the Messiah, through whom also we have obtained our introduction by faith into this grace in which we stand; and we exult in hope of the glory of God. And not only this, but we also exult in our tribulations, knowing that tribulation brings about perseverance; and perseverance, proven character; and proven character, hope."

Notice that Paul says that Believers are to "exult in our present sufferings, because we know that suffering trains us to endure" (NEB). The Greek verb for "boast" or "exult" is *kauchaomai* (καυχάομαι), specifically meaning, "*to speak loud, be loud-tongued*" (*LS*).[25] The NIV says to "rejoice in our sufferings." While this does speak of "tribulation" perhaps in the context of being persecuted as a Believer, where is any allusion to any kind of escape from it, much less a pre-tribulation rapture escape? You will not find it.

The second reference offered says,

> "Now as to the times and the epochs, brethren, you have no need of anything to be written to you. For you yourselves know full well that the day of the Lord will come just like a thief in the night. While they are saying, 'Peace and safety!' then destruction will come upon them suddenly like labor pains upon a woman with child, and they will not escape. But you, brethren, are not in darkness, that the day would overtake you like a thief; for you are all sons of light and sons of day. We are not of night nor of darkness; so then let us not sleep as others do, but let us be alert and sober. For those who sleep do their sleeping at night, and those who get drunk get drunk at night. But since we are of *the* day, let us be sober, having put on the breastplate of faith and love, and as a helmet, the hope of salvation. For God has not destined us for wrath, but for obtaining salvation through our Lord Yeshua the Messiah" (1 Thessalonians 5:1-9).

---

[25] *LS*, 424.

We have already addressed this passage previously as well. It is important to note that the context of being spared from "wrath" here is being on guard as it concerns the Day of the LORD or *Yom-ADONAI* (יוֹם־יְהוָה), when God's final judgment is poured out on Planet Earth before the inauguration of the Millennium. The context of Paul's writing the Thessalonicans is for Believers to be continually on watch. He admonishes them, "let us be alert and self-controlled" (NIV). This is not in the context of an any-moment, pre-tribulation rapture escape, but rather regards the Day of the LORD and the final judgment on the world prior to Yeshua's appearing. This Day of the LORD comes unexpectedly to those who are unaware—which should understandably *not include* faithful Believers who are on guard and not going to be overtaken like a thief. With this information, we can now properly understand Revelation 6:14-17:

> "The sky was split apart like a scroll when it is rolled up, and every mountain and island were moved out of their places. Then the kings of the earth and the great men and the commanders and the rich and the strong and every slave and free man hid themselves in the caves and among the rocks of the mountains; and they said to the mountains and to the rocks, 'Fall on us and hide us from the presence of Him who sits on the throne, and from the wrath of the Lamb; for the great day of their wrath has come, and who is able to stand?'"

It is notable to point out that the Day of the LORD or *Yom-ADONAI* is a time which occurs in conjunction with the post-tribulational gathering of the saints, as Yeshua says in Matthew 24:29, "Immediately after the suffering of those days the sun will be darkened, and the moon will not give its light; the stars will fall from heaven, and the powers of heaven will be shaken" (NRSV). This includes quotations or allusions from some critical Day of the LORD prophecies in the Tanach (Isaiah 13:10; Ezekiel

32:7; Joel 2:10, 31; 3:15),[26] each of which places or points to *Yom-ADONAI* as occurring or climaxing at the conclusion of the Great Tribulation, most likely culminating on a future Day of Atonement or *Yom Kippur*,[27] and not occurring during the entire Seventieth Week of Israel as falsely implied by pre-tribulationists. Take important note of the array of these prophecies in light of the Messiah's words:

> "Wail, for the day of the LORD is near! It will come as destruction from the Almighty...For the stars of heaven and their constellations will not flash forth their light; the sun will be dark when it rises and the moon will not shed its light...Therefore I will make the heavens tremble, and the earth will be shaken from its place at the fury of the LORD of hosts in the day of His burning anger" (Isaiah 13:6, 10, 13).

> "And when *I* extinguish you, I will cover the heavens and darken their stars; I will cover the sun with a cloud and the moon will not give its light" (Ezekiel 32:7).

> "Before them the earth quakes, the heavens tremble, the sun and the moon grow dark and the stars lose their brightness. The LORD utters His voice before His army; surely His camp is very great, for strong is he who carries out His word. The day of the LORD is indeed great and very awesome, and who can endure it?" (Joel 2:10-11).

> "The sun will be turned into darkness and the moon into blood before the great and awesome day of the LORD comes" (Joel 2:31).

> "Multitudes, multitudes in the valley of decision! For the day of the LORD is near in the valley of decision. The sun and moon grow dark and the stars lose their brightness" (Joel 3:14-15).

---

[26] Kurt Aland, et. al., *The Greek New Testament, Fourth Revised Edition* (Stuttgart: Deutche Bibelgesellschaft/United Bible Societies, 1998), 94.
[27] For further comments on the prophetic significance of *Yom Kippur*, consult the *Fall Holiday Helper* by TNN Press.

14. The church will not be overtaken by the Day of the Lord (1 Thes. 5:1-9) which includes the tribulation.

We have answered this claim in Walvoord's previous proof for pre-tribulationism. We have shown that the Day of the LORD occurs in conjunction with the post-tribulational gathering of the saints—the point when His significant judgment is unleashed upon the rebels of Planet Earth—when properly connected to Matthew 24:29 and Yeshua's quotations or allusions to Isaiah 13:10; Ezekiel 32:7; Joel 2:10, 31; 3:15. Even when considering the likelihood of the Day of the LORD being more of a period of time, than a specific twenty-four hour "day," claiming that it includes the entire Seventieth Week of Israel is an incorrect conclusion to draw.

15. The possibility of a believer escaping the tribulation is mentioned in Luke 21:36.

Let us examine what Luke 21:36 actually tells us: "But keep on the alert at all times, praying that you may have strength to escape all these things that are about to take place, and to stand before the Son of Man."

In most Bibles, the Greek verb *ekpheugō* (ἐκφεύγω) is rendered as "escape,"[28] but it can also be legitimately translated "flee." *BDAG* defines *ekpheugō* as both "**to seek safety in flight, *run away*"** and "**to become free from danger by avoiding some peril, *escape*."**[29] The REB actually renders Luke 21:36 with, "Be on the alert, praying at all times for strength to **pass safely through** [*ekpheugō*] all that is coming." The proper usage of *ekpheugō* is speaking of fleeing from a place or a situation, not being completely removed from the Tribulation period. Yeshua the Messiah tells His followers to remain on guard so that they might be able to flee from all of the

---

[28] Including, but not limited to: KJV, RSV, NASU, NIV, NKJV, LITV, NRSV, NLT, ESV.
[29] *BDAG*, 312.

situations, persecutions, and catastrophes of Daniel's Seventieth Week—not be removed via the pre-tribulation rapture.

Interestingly enough, the verb translated as "have strength" in this passage is *katischuō* (κατισχύω), and fully means, "*to have power over, overpower, prevail against one*" or "*to come to one's full strength*" (*LS*).[30] If we are admonished by the Lord to have strength to overcome and prevail, where is the implication of a pre-tribulation rapture? The escapist motives of pre-tribulationists should be obvious here. The Book of Revelation, in contrast to this, begins with multiple words to the saints, encouraging them to overcome (Revelation 2:7, 11, 17, 26; 3:5, 12, 21).

16. The church of Philadelphia was promised deliverance from "the hour of trial, that hour which is to come upon the whole world, to try them that dwell upon the earth" (Rev. 3:10).

We have already discussed this pre-tribulational claim previously, but it is important that we reemphasize it again. The two critical mistakes made by pre-tribulationists here are: (1) this promise is made to the assembly of Philadelphia, not all of the seven assemblies of Revelation, and (2) the hour of trial or temptation is assumed to be the Tribulation period.

Revelation 3:10 in its entirety states, "Because you have kept the word of My perseverance, I also will keep you from the hour of testing, that *hour* which is about to come upon the whole world, to test those who dwell on the earth." This promise is only given to those who keep the word of Yeshua's patience or *hupomonē* (ὑπομονή), meaning "*a holding out, patient endurance*" (*LS*).[31] Those Believers who compose the assembly of Philadelphia are patient concerning their Master's return, as opposed to

---

[30] *LS*, 423.
[31] Ibid., 845.

looking for the rapture or the start of the Great Tribulation around every corner. Furthermore, the hour of *peirasmos* (πειρασμός) specifically concerns "the temptation by which the devil sought to divert Jesus the Messiah from his divine errand" (*Thayer*).[32] Yeshua was tempted in the wilderness by Satan to worship him and thus be given all the kingdoms of the world (Matthew 4:1; Mark 1:13; Luke 4:2). The key temptation of the Tribulation is similar:

"And it was given to him to give breath to the image of the beast, so that the image of the beast would even speak and cause as many as do not worship the image of the beast to be killed" (Revelation 13:15).

Those who refuse to receive the mark of the beast and worship the antimessiah/antichrist will be executed. I believe this is the hour of trial or temptation that the Philadelphian Believers during the Seventieth Week of Israel will be spared from. This notably does not include everyone, but just those who classify as being Philadelphian.[33] They will have the ability to flee from this trial (cf. Luke 21:36).

17. It is characteristic of divine dealing to deliver believers before a divine judgment is inflicted upon the world as illustrated in the deliverance of Noah, Lot, Rahab, etc. (2 Pet. 2:6-9).

2 Peter 2:6-9 is provided as evidence to support the belief that a "deliverance," by extension meaning some kind of a "removal," must occur prior to the Tribulation period. Let us examine these verses in their entirety, so we know that we are properly applying the Tanach (Old Testament) typology. As the Apostle Peter asserts,

---

[32] *Thayer*, 498.
[33] For a further discussion, consult Chapter 3 of *When Will the Messiah Return?*: "The Seven Assemblies of Revelation, and the Philadelphian Congregation."

"[A]nd [God] did not spare the ancient world, but preserved Noah, a preacher of righteousness, with seven others, when He brought a flood upon the world of the ungodly; and *if* He condemned the cities of Sodom and Gomorrah to destruction by reducing *them* to ashes, having made them an example to those who would live ungodly *lives* thereafter; and *if* He rescued righteous Lot, oppressed by the sensual conduct of unprincipled men (for by what he saw and heard *that* righteous man, while living among them, felt *his* righteous soul tormented day after day by *their* lawless deeds), *then* the Lord knows how to rescue the godly from temptation, and to keep the unrighteous under punishment for the day of judgment" (2 Peter 2:5-9).

It is very true that the Lord did indeed provide deliverance to Noah, Lot, and Rahab—the three Biblical characters specifically mentioned—prior to the Flood, the destruction of Sodom and Gomorrah, and the conquering of Jericho by the Ancient Israelites. But is this a conclusive proof for pre-tribulationism? Let us review what the Tanach (Old Testament) actually tells us about the judgment, and thus *when* the deliverance of these people actually took place.

Noah and the Flood

The account of Noah is the first example given in support of the pre-tribulation rapture. It is important for us to properly understand the story of Noah, because Yeshua says, "As it was in the days of Noah, so it will be at the coming of the Son of Man" (Matthew 24:37, NIV). What occurred during the Flood of Genesis chs. 6-8 is going to repeat itself in some capacity.

As a backdrop to the Flood, we are first told that "Noah was five hundred years old, and Noah became the father of Shem, Ham, and Japheth" (Genesis 5:32). It is important to know what Noah's age was here, because "Noah was six hundred years old when the flood of water came upon the earth. Then Noah and his sons and his wife and his sons' wives with him entered the ark because of the water of the flood" (Genesis 7:6-7). Interestingly enough, *The Bible Knowledge Commentary*,

Old Testament edited by Walvoord and Roy B. Zuck, states (Genesis commentary by Allen P. Ross) the following in regard to the time gap between Noah's sons being born at his age of 500, and then the Flood coming when he was 600: "Even though swift judgment would fall because God's Spirit would not always shield...mankind, the judgment would be delayed 120 years (v. 3). During this time Noah was 'a preacher of righteousness' (2 Peter 2:5)."[34]

This belief of a delay of 120 years is based on an interpretation of God's words in Genesis 6:3: "My Spirit shall not strive with man forever, because he also is flesh; nevertheless his days shall be one hundred and twenty years." While there are varying views of this verse, we see that there was about a century between Noah's sons being born and the Flood occurring. This period was the time when Noah prepared for the judgment, building the ark and preparing it for the animals which would be carried by it. 2 Peter 2:5 tells us that Noah was "a herald of righteousness" (RSV). The specific Greek word often mistranslated "preacher" is *kērux* (κῆρυξ), actually meaning "*a herald, pursuivant, marshal, public messenger.*" In its secular context it meant "*a crier, who* made proclamation in the public assemblies" *(LS)*.[35]

While Noah was not a "preacher" in the modern sense of the word, Noah did warn others of the impending judgment to come during the proposed 100-120 years, at the very least by his actions of obedience to God. Sadly, the parallel today is that many pre-tribulationists do not often emphasize the judgment of God upon the world and the required repentance from fallen human beings, but instead emphasize escape and their inability to endure through (any) difficult times. Noah prepared himself and his family for the judgment

---

[34] Allen P. Ross, "Genesis," in John F. Walvoord and Roy B. Zuck, *The Bible Knowledge Commentary, Old Testament* (Wheaton, IL: Victor Books, 1985), 37.

[35] *LS*, 432.

that was to come, and then at the very end of the preparations—*at the very last moment*—the Flood came:

"In the six hundredth year of Noah's life, in the second month, on the seventeenth day of the month, on the same day all the fountains of the great deep burst open, and the floodgates of the sky were opened. The rain fell upon the earth for forty days and forty nights. On the very same day Noah and Shem and Ham and Japheth, the sons of Noah, and Noah's wife and the three wives of his sons with them, entered the ark, they and every beast after its kind, and all the cattle after their kind, and every creeping thing that creeps on the earth after its kind, and every bird after its kind, all sorts of birds. So they went into the ark to Noah, by twos of all flesh in which was the breath of life. Those that entered, male and female of all flesh, entered as God had commanded him; and the LORD closed *it* behind him" (Genesis 7:11-16).

Was Noah "raptured" as many pre-tribulationists like to imply? No, he was not. Noah was kept safe by the Lord in the ark that He had commanded him to build. Noah was fully aware of the floodwaters around him while in the massive boat. The Orthodox Jewish *ArtScroll Chumash* actually indicates, "The Sages add that the waters were scalding hot."[36] Whether this is true or not—and I am inclined to regard this as complete speculation—Noah knew the tribulation going on around him as the world of sinful humanity was being wiped out:

"Then the flood came upon the earth for forty days, and the water increased and lifted up the ark, so that it rose above the earth. The water prevailed and increased greatly upon the earth, and the ark floated on the surface of the water" (Genesis 7:17-18).

Knowing this is crucial to understanding Yeshua's words in Matthew 24:37-39:

"For the coming of the Son of Man will be just like the days of Noah. For as in those days before the flood

---

[36] Nosson Scherman, ed., *ArtScroll Chumash, Stone Edition* (Brooklyn: Mesorah Publications, Ltd., 2000), 35; cf. b.*Sanhedrin*108b.

they were eating and drinking, marrying and giving in marriage, until the day that Noah entered the ark, and they did not understand until the flood came and took them all away; so will the coming of the Son of Man be."

When we understand that Noah was preparing himself and his family for around a century prior to the Flood, and the Messiah's words where He says that people were going on as normal until the Flood came and took them away, then we can see how claiming Noah as a type of the pre-tribulation rapture has poor support. Noah was removed from the scene at the very last possible moment, not long before the final judgment. Those taken away were not brought up to Heaven, but were swept away in judgment by the Flood—suddenly and swiftly. This is important to recognize because when Yeshua arrives, His return will be swift and sudden to those not paying attention, or purposefully ignoring the signs, and they will be judged suddenly—just like those in the Flood! Believers will be taken up to safety above the judgment at the Messiah's appearing, right before He returns to the Earth.

Sodom and Gomorrah

The second example given for a pre-tribulation rapture is the story of Lot and how he was removed from the judgment upon Sodom and Gomorrah. This too is very important because Yeshua alludes to it in Luke 17:28-30 in regard to the Last Days and His return:

"It was the same as happened in the days of Lot: they were eating, they were drinking, they were buying, they were selling, they were planting, they were building; but on the day that Lot went out from Sodom it rained fire and brimstone from heaven and destroyed them all. It will be just the same on the day that the Son of Man is revealed."

Prior to the Lord destroying the cities of Sodom and Gomorrah, which were debauched with problems of extreme homosexuality, Abraham pleads for God not to judge them. He pleads that if specific numbers of righteous persons be found within the cities that the judgment be spared:

"So the LORD said, 'If I find in Sodom fifty righteous within the city, then I will spare the whole place on their account.' And Abraham replied, 'Now behold, I have ventured to speak to the Lord, although I am *but* dust and ashes. Suppose the fifty righteous are lacking five, will You destroy the whole city because of five?' And He said, 'I will not destroy *it* if I find forty-five there.' He spoke to Him yet again and said, 'Suppose forty are found there?' And He said, 'I will not do *it* on account of the forty.' Then he said, 'Oh may the Lord not be angry, and I shall speak; suppose thirty are found there?' And He said, 'I will not do *it* if I find thirty there.' And he said, 'Now behold, I have ventured to speak to the Lord; suppose twenty are found there?' And He said, 'I will not destroy *it* on account of the twenty.' Then he said, 'Oh may the Lord not be angry, and I shall speak only this once; suppose ten are found there?' And He said, 'I will not destroy *it* on account of the ten'" (Genesis 18:26-32).

Unfortunately, ten righteous were not found in the cities of Sodom and Gomorrah. Lawlessness—in the true sense of the word—reigned supreme in these places. As a result, the Lord sent two angels to Lot for him and his family to evacuate the city immediately. Notice that Lot was not entirely enthusiastic about the messengers' visit, and asked them to spend the night at his house and then for them to go on their way. Does this non-enthusiasm picture many Believers who are awaiting the Second Coming of the Lord? How many people would rather be in the world, than enter into the new world of peace and true harmony which is awaiting in God's Kingdom on Earth?

"Now the two angels came to Sodom in the evening as Lot was sitting in the gate of Sodom. When Lot saw *them*, he rose to meet them and bowed down *with his* face to the ground. And he said, 'Now behold, my lords, please turn aside into your servant's house, and spend the night, and wash your feet; then you may rise early and go on your way.' They said however, 'No, but we shall spend the night in the square'" (Genesis 19:1-2).

We know that after Lot greets the angels and brings them into his house, the men of Sodom become anxious and want Lot to present these two men to them so they might "know them" (Genesis 19:5). Instead, Lot offers them his two virgin daughters, whom they refuse (Genesis 19:7-8). The men become rowdy and "they pressed hard against Lot and came near to break the door" of his house (Genesis 19:9). Already, we must ask where the implication of a pre-tribulation rapture is. It seems that the sin and lawlessness are so surrounding Lot and his family that they are just going to have to get out while they still have a chance—not like the pre-trib scenario of the rapture occurring and only then sin and lawlessness abounding.

At the breaking point, the men of Sodom—the Sodomites—try to break into Lot's house:

"Then the *two* men said to Lot, 'Whom else have you here? A son-in-law, and your sons, and your daughters, and whomever you have in the city, bring *them* out of the place; or we are about to destroy this place, because their outcry has become so great before the LORD that the LORD has sent us to destroy it'" (Genesis 19:12-13).

At the very last moment Lot is delivered by the angels from the judgment to befall Sodom. He is not removed from the city seven days prior to the destruction being poured out. In fact, we are told, "But he hesitated. So the men seized his hand and the hand of his wife and the hands of his two daughters, for the compassion of the LORD *was* upon him; and they brought him out, and put him outside the city. When they had brought them outside, one said, 'Escape for your life! Do not look behind you, and do not stay anywhere in the valley; escape to the mountains, or you will be swept away'" (Genesis 19:16-17). Before the angels forcibly remove him from the city, "Still he delayed" (NJPS).

Of course, we know what happens. As they leave the city Lot's wife looks back and is turned into a pillar of salt:

"The sun had risen over the earth when Lot came to Zoar. Then the LORD rained on Sodom and Gomorrah brimstone and fire from the LORD out of heaven, and He overthrew those cities, and all the valley, and all the inhabitants of the cities, and what grew on the ground. But his wife, from behind him, looked *back*, and she became a pillar of salt" (Genesis 19:23-26).

Lot's wife lingered and could not keep up with the rest of her family. Why was this the case? Was it because of all she was leaving behind in Sodom? Was it because she could not leave her possessions? Some have speculated that she not only looked back on Sodom, but actually ran *into the city* as the judgment was falling. We may never know the exact answer, but it is important for us to realize that the reason why so many Believers are unexcited about the return of Yeshua is because of what they will have to give up and leave behind in regard to their Earthly lives and possessions. It is for this reason why the Messiah says the following in Luke 17:31-33:

"On that day, the one who is on the housetop and whose goods are in the house must not go down to take them out; and likewise the one who is in the field must not turn back. Remember Lot's wife. Whoever seeks to keep his life will lose it, and whoever loses *his life* will preserve it."

When properly understanding the story of Lot, there is no support for the pre-tribulation rapture in it at all. Lot is removed from Sodom at the very last moment prior to the judgment occurring. He is not removed a substantial amount of time *before* the judgment as pre-tribulationism would imply. The text speaks of a sudden judgment and would allude to Believers being removed from Planet Earth just prior to the Day of the LORD or *Yom-ADONAI* occurring.

Rahab and the Fall of Jericho
The third example given is that of Rahab, the prostitute from Jericho who assisted the Israelite spies in their defeat of the city. Rahab was spared from the judgment which was to befall Jericho, but does her

deliverance from the attack give us any reason to believe in a pre-tribulation rapture? Joshua 6:12-14 tells us the following concerning what happened *prior* to the attack on Jericho:

"Now Joshua rose early in the morning, and the priests took up the ark of the LORD. The seven priests carrying the seven trumpets of rams' horns before the ark of the LORD went on continually, and blew the trumpets; and the armed men went before them and the rear guard came after the ark of the LORD, while they continued to blow the trumpets. Thus the second day they marched around the city once and returned to the camp; they did so for six days."

The people of Jericho were given adequate warning that the Israelites were going to attack. The priests carried the Ark of the Covenant and blew *shofar*s marching around the city for a period of six days. On the seventh day the Israelites attacked:

"Then on the seventh day they rose early at the dawning of the day and marched around the city in the same manner seven times; only on that day they marched around the city seven times. At the seventh time, when the priests blew the trumpets, Joshua said to the people, 'Shout! For the LORD has given you the city. The city shall be under the ban, it and all that is in it belongs to the LORD; only Rahab the harlot and all who are with her in the house shall live, because she hid the messengers whom we sent'" (Joshua 6:15-17).

It is very interesting that the attack upon Jericho occurred on the seventh day. If the seven days are a type of the Seventieth Week of Israel, then it indicates that the Final Battle occurs in the last part of this time period. The people of Jericho, representing the people of the world, are given an adequate warning by the people of God. But only Rahab and her family are spared, and the rest are defeated:

"So the young men who were spies went in and brought out Rahab and her father and her mother and her brothers and all she had; they also brought out all her relatives and placed them outside the camp of Israel.

They burned the city with fire, and all that was in it. Only the silver and gold, and articles of bronze and iron, they put into the treasury of the house of the LORD. However, Rahab the harlot and her father's household and all she had, Joshua spared; and she has lived in the midst of Israel to this day, for she hid the messengers whom Joshua sent to spy out Jericho" (Joshua 6:23-25).

The story of Rahab does not picture any kind of pre-tribulation rapture of the saints. Rather, it indicates once again that right before the final judgment comes, God's people will be removed. And in this case, the major judgment comes on the seventh, or last day, out of a period of seven—not on the first.

Summary

After reviewing the records of Noah, Lot, and Rahab, is the premise of Believers being removed prior to Divine judgment valid? Yes and no. Yes, in the sense that Believers are removed from Divine judgment, as the judgments Noah, Lot, and Rahab were spared from are each a legitimate foreshadowing of the future Day of the LORD. No, in that they are not removed *long before* this final judgment occurs. Each one of them was removed at the very last moment, and those judged were given an adequate time to know what was to befall them. The pattern is not for Believers to be removed, then for the world to continue on not knowing what is coming, and then for sinners to finally be judged. The accounts of Noah, Lot, and Rahab should teach Messiah followers to be ready to be removed from the scene at the last minute.

18. At the time of the translation of the church, all believers go to the Father's house in heaven (John 14:3), and do not immediately return to the earth after meeting Christ in the air as posttribulationists teach.

In this proof for pre-tribulationism, there is likely an allusion to what many pre-tribulationists call the "Jewish

Marriage Analogy," a teaching where Believers are taken into Heaven prior to the Tribulation period to consummate "the marriage" for seven years. This teaching is largely taught by Messianic pre-tribulationists, and then has been picked up by many Christian pre-tribulationists. Since we are post-tribulational and Messianic, some find it perplexing why we reject this teaching as having legitimacy. Perhaps it is because most Christians who accept it, *and who claim to have "embraced" their Hebraic Roots,* usually reject core Messianic positions such as the continued validity of the Torah, and the Messianic lifestyle including keeping the seventh-day Sabbath, the appointed times of Leviticus 23, and following the kosher dietary laws—and instead believe in a teaching that is not directly spoken of in Scripture. I made the following observations in *When Will the Messiah Return?*:

> There is, however, one so-called "Hebraic truth" which many of today's Christians—pre-tribulationists who study prophecy—eagerly embrace. They call it the "Jewish Marriage Analogy." It is ironic, but while largely rejecting, or at least not considering, the Biblically-prescribed festivals and commandments that the Lord has instilled for His people in the Torah— which should enable us to more properly and better understand His plan of redemption (Colossians 2:17)— many think that "the Church" will be raptured to Heaven and be married with Yeshua on the basis of marriage customs of First Century Israel. On the one hand, these Christians will often have very little, or nothing, to do with what the Torah and Tanakh says about how God's people should conduct themselves— but on the other, they widely embrace something that is largely not talked about in Scripture, and is not necessarily confirmed by history, either.
>
> The presupposition of the "Jewish Marriage Analogy" is that "the Church" is the "Bride of Messiah," and is thus eagerly awaiting a marriage to her Lord. Pre-tribulationists commonly teach that "the Bride" would never be subject to the horrors of the Great Tribulation and must be removed from the Seventieth Week of Israel, so God "can deal with the Jews." While the Bride is in Heaven consummating the marriage, pre-

tribulationists advocate that Israel or the Jewish people
will be on Earth experiencing the Tribulation.[37]

The "Jewish Marriage Analogy" teaching has been
addressed in Chapter 6 of *When Will the Messiah Return?*,
"Who or What is the True Bride of Messiah?" This
chapter considers the problems of accepting something
that is not explicitly taught in the Bible, and ignoring
some key passages which tell us what the Father's House
truly is, which is ultimately not located in Heaven.

I will briefly comment on "the Father's House" and
the "place" that Yeshua is preparing for His own.
Walvoord references John 14:2-3 as a support for pre-
tribulationism, and the idea that we are to be taken into
the Father's House prior to the Tribulation period:

"In My Father's house are many dwelling places; if it
were not so, I would have told you; for I go to prepare a
place for you. If I go and prepare a place for you, I will
come again and receive you to Myself, that where I am,
there you may be also."

By quoting this, pre-tribulationists tell us that Yeshua
is presently in Heaven preparing a marriage residence for
us, and one day the Father will tell Him to gather the
saints to "consummate the marriage" prior to the
Tribulation period. But is this really what He is saying?

First of all, Yeshua tells us that in His "Father's house
are many dwelling places." The verb *eisin* (εἰσιν) appears
in the present active indicative tense, indicating that
these dwelling places presently are in Heaven. This
implies that if any of us die in the faith, we have some
kind of a domicile waiting for us in Heaven for us where
we can rest and be refreshed until the resurrection.[38]
Yeshua does not need to go and "create them."

Secondly, can we assume that the Father's house is
exclusively Heaven? The Messiah referred to His "Father's

---

[37] McKee, *WWTMR*, 138.
[38] Cf. N.T. Wright, *Surprised by Hope: Rethinking Heaven, the
Resurrection, and the Mission of the Church* (New York: HarperCollins,
2008), 41.

house" as the Temple in John 2:15-17. Throughout the Hebrew Tanach there are passages which refer to this house, which is "the house of the LORD" or *beit ADONAI* (בֵּית יְהוָה). It includes the Tabernacle in the wilderness (1 Samuel 1:24), Solomon's Temple (2 Chronicles 2:1; 7:16), and the future Millennial Temple (Isaiah 2:2-4; Joel 3:18). Furthermore, the *ekklēsia* or assembly of Believers is allegorically understood to be "the Temple" (Ephesians 2:19-22).

But what of the "place" that we are told the Messiah is "preparing" for us? If it is not a "marriage residence," then what is it?

The Greek word translated "place" in this passage is *topos* (τόπος). While generally used in the Apostolic Scriptures to refer to a physical location, it nevertheless has a variety of additional usages. In usages outside of the Bible "*tópos* sometimes means 'sanctuary' (the holy place)...Another use is for 'someone's place,' e.g., a senator's seat, a place at school, one's place in the world" (*TDNT*).[39] Is the place Yeshua is preparing for us a "marriage chamber"? Or, is the Messiah preparing **a place of authority** for us in His Father's Kingdom? After all, are we not told that "we will be *cohanim* [priests] of God and of the Messiah, and...will rule with him for the thousand years" (Revelation 20:6, CJB)? What is the "place" that Yeshua is really preparing for His followers?

The Messiah is presently not in Heaven preparing a marriage residence for us as pre-tribulationists commonly tell us. He is, however, in Heaven readying our stations or places of authority for His coming Earthly Kingdom. The Scriptures are replete with admonitions how we are to be responsible Believers here in this world so that the Lord can reward us in His future Kingdom in the world to come.[40]

---

[39] H. Köster, "*tópos*," in *TDNT*, 1184.
[40] Consult the further discussion on John 14:2-3 in the author's publication, *To Be Absent From the Body*.

19. Pretribulationism does not divide the body of Christ at the rapture on a works principle. The teaching of a partial rapture is based on the false doctrine that the translation of the church is a reward for good works. It is rather a climatic aspect of salvation by grace.

As a post-tribulationist, I have never argued in favor of a "partial rapture" whereas one sector of the Body of Messiah is removed from the difficulties of the Tribulation period, and others must endure this hardship. But as a Messianic, who believes in the continued validity of the Torah for Believers today, I do believe that good works and obedience to God are evidence of a true salvation experience. While we are all saved by God's grace, good works are to be a manifestation of such inward grace (Ephesians 2:8-10). James the Just plainly says, "Even so faith, if it has no works, is dead, *being* by itself. But someone may *well* say, 'You have faith and I have works; show me your faith without the works, and I will show you my faith by my works'" (James 2:17-18).[41]

Most pre-tribulationists strongly believe that in some way the Torah has been abolished by Yeshua the Messiah, or has been put aside for the Church Age, and frequently their idea of "grace" is not a Biblical one—as it may be a grace without responsibility. We know that by studying the patterns given for us in the Torah such as the Exodus of the Ancient Israelites out of Egypt and the trials they endured in the wilderness, that there is no previous Biblical pattern given for a pre-tribulation rapture. While God's grace covers our sins and our faults, as Believers in Messiah Yeshua we are called to be responsible, and a part of this responsibility means enduring for our faith—even if we are called to experience the Seventieth Week of Israel.

---

[41] Please note that these "works" in the Jamean context are primarily works of grace and mercy. Consult the author's commentary *James for the Practical Messianic* for a further discussion.

20. The Scripture clearly teaches that all, not part, of the church will be raptured at the coming of Christ for the church (1 Cor. 15:51-52).

This argument is directed at partial rapturists and not at post-tribulationists. While we disagree with the pre-tribulationists that God has two groups of elect, Israel and "the Church," and that He has only one called out assembly, the community of Israel, of which all Believers are a part—I have always believed that all of the *qahal/ekklēsia* of the redeemed will be gathered to meet Yeshua in the clouds all at once. There will be no "series of gatherings" of the saints, as partial rapturists believe, but one single gathering of Believers into the clouds. Paul makes this quite clear:

"Behold, I tell you a mystery; we will not all sleep, but **we will all be changed,**[42] in a moment, in the twinkling of an eye, at the last trumpet; for the trumpet will sound, and the dead will be raised imperishable, and we will be changed" (1 Corinthians 15:51-52).

Of course, it is interesting that 1 Corinthians 15:51-52 is referenced as a proof that all will be changed. This verse points the gathering of the saints at "the last trumpet," which is hardly a support for a pre-tribulation rapture. Somehow this "last" trumpet is believed by pre-tribulationists to actually be first and not connected to the seventh trumpet of Revelation. No Scriptural support is given for this; it is just said to be a separate event. Why?

21. As opposed to a view of partial rapture, pretribulationism is founded on the definite teaching of Scripture that the death of Christ frees us from all condemnation.

While this argument is specifically targeted at partial rapturists, it is likewise targeted at post-tribulationists, as

---

[42] Grk. *pantes de allagēsometha* (πάντες δὲ ἀλλαγησόμεθα).

being subject to "condemnation" is by implication having to experience the Tribulation period. Romans 8:1 astutely tells us, "There is therefore now no condemnation for those who are in Messiah Yeshua." This is no doubt the specific passage being referred to. It is notable that if one reviews the context of the following verses, this text is not speaking of the Tribulation period at all, but of the penalties that born again Believers have been freed from by experiencing salvation and redemption from sin. Romans 8:1-2 states in its entirety,

"Therefore there is now no condemnation for those who are in Messiah Yeshua. For the law of the Spirit of life in Messiah Yeshua has set you free from the law of sin and of death."

In these two verses, the Apostle Paul is likely contrasting two spiritual laws or constants. If you sin you are subject to death or eternal separation from God; however, the Spirit of life in Messiah Yeshua brings the redeemed into communion with the Father and frees them from the penalty of eternal punishment. This is not a promise not to be subject to tribulation, be it general persecution or the Seventieth Week of Israel.

Yeshua Himself says in John 16:33, "These things I have spoken to you, so that in Me you may have peace. In the world you have tribulation, but take courage; I have overcome the world." Because of our faith in Him, we are guaranteed to experience "trouble" (NIV) or "persecution" (NRSV). Interestingly enough, Paul says further in Romans 8, "Who will separate us from the love of Messiah? Will tribulation, or distress, or persecution, or famine, or nakedness, or peril, or sword?" (v. 35). Truly, if we are in Him, **it will not matter if we face the Tribulation.**

The condemnation spoken of here is not the Tribulation period, but is instead "the law of sin and death," the spiritual constant that guarantees people eternal punishment if they disobey God and are unrepentant. The horrors of the Seventieth Week of Israel, while severe and sobering, are not "condemnation." Take to serious heart the reality that

Messiah Yeshua tells His followers to "Be courageous! I have conquered the world" (John 16:33, HCSB). If our faith and trust are in Him, regardless of what happens, we have nothing to fear.

22. The godly remnant of the tribulation are pictured as Israelites, not members of the church as maintained by posttribulationists.

The godly remnant of the Tribulation period are pictured as being members of Israel. These Believers, notably, are "saints who keep the commandments of God and [have] faith in Yeshua" (Revelation 14:12; 12:17). In our day, many Messianic Believers—not only Jewish Believers, but also non-Jewish Believers—are taking this prophecy to serious heart, as they endeavor to truly have the faith of Messiah Yeshua[43] and observe the commandments of God in the Torah. Of the pre-tribulationists who claim that this is not speaking of them, we can only ask: **You do not have the testimony of Yeshua the Messiah (Jesus Christ) and do not keep** (any of?) **God's commandments?**

Of course, it is notable that many post-tribulationists in the past have had some serious problems with this admonition from Revelation as well. Many Christian post-tribulationists, or at least those of the past, have falsely believed in replacement theology, as opposed to believing that God's promises to Israel, to regather the descendants of Abraham, Isaac, and Jacob back to the Holy Land, remain true. Many also falsely believe, just as most Christian pre-tribulationists, that the Torah has been entirely abolished by Yeshua, so they have a problem with this remnant keeping the "commandments

---

[43] Alternatively, the genitive clause *tēn pistin Iēsou* (τὴν πίστιν Ἰησοῦ) could be understood as "the faithfulness of Jesus," meaning our Lord's obedience to the Father, to die on behalf of sinful humanity.

For a further discussion, consult the author's article "The Faithfulness of Yeshua the Messiah."

of God," a definite reference to the Torah or Law of Moses.

Fortunately, much of the Messianic community today rightly emphasizes that all Believers are a part of the Commonwealth of Israel. The end-time remnant is indeed composed of Believers in Yeshua the Messiah, be they Jewish or non-Jewish, recognizing Him as Savior and properly obeying the commandments.

23. The pretribulational view as opposed to posttribulationism does not confuse general terms like elect and saints which apply to the saved of all ages with specific terms like church and those in Christ which refer to believers of this age only.

This support for pre-tribulationism is where most pre-tribulationists' dispensational bias, which separates Israel and the so-called "Church," should be apparent. Because pre-tribulationists believe that Israel and "the Church" are separate groups of elect, they likewise believe that when the "elect" or the "saints" are referred to in particular Scripture passages, that it is not speaking to *all the elect* or *all saints*. Furthermore, they downplay the reality that the Greek word *ekklēsia*, most often translated in Bibles as "church," is connected to the Hebrew word *qahal* referencing Israel via the Septuagint. The reality is that if the *ekklēsia* referred to in the Apostolic Scriptures is indeed the community of Israel, which has incorporated non-Jewish Believers into its polity, then their pre-tribulational arguments of "the Church" being taken to Heaven prior to the Tribulation period, largely fail.

I have addressed the argument of there not being a separate "Church—and instead all Believers being a part of Israel—in related books and articles. What makes this understanding controversial more than anything else is its applications to one's theology *and* lifestyle. A major part of the theological application is the fact that when you recognize yourself as a part of Israel, it forces you to reject the pre-tribulation rapture, because Israel experiences the Seventieth Week of Israel or Tribulation period. Another major application is that Israel is called to follow the Torah or Law of Moses, which much of mainstream Christianity today largely and falsely believes was totally abolished by Yeshua the Messiah (and is indeed suffering from this omission spiritually and morally, unfortunately).

DOCTRINE OF IMMINENCY?

24. The pretribulational interpretation is the only view which teaches that the coming of Christ is actually imminent.

The idea that the coming of the Messiah is "imminent," meaning that it can occur at any moment for all Believers, as most pre-tribulationists attest, is based on their interpretation of Yeshua's words where He says that we will not know the day or the hour of His return:

"But of that day or hour no one knows, not even the angels in heaven, nor the Son, but the Father *alone*" (Mark 13:32; cf. Matthew 24:36).

Pre-tribulationists take this admonition of Yeshua's and then proceed to tell us that the Messiah can return at any moment, and that there are no major prophetic events that must occur prior to His return; He can simply return at any moment. This is not a very responsible reading of the Biblical text. The Lord says that we will not know the "day or hour," and this is a reference to the *exact time* of His return. The Greek verb rendered as "knows" is *oida* (οἶδα), and specifically means "**to grasp the meaning of someth.,** *understand, recognize, come to know, experience*" (*BDAG*).[44] So when Yeshua says that no one knows the day or the hour, what is He really communicating? He is not only telling His followers that

---

[44] *BDAG*, 694.

thoy cannot know the exact time of His return, but they cannot fully understand what it means until it takes place—as this is something that the Father Himself only knows, as He is the One who has fixed the times (Acts 1:7). Yeshua the Messiah is certainly *not* saying that He can just "show up" at any moment.

It is correct that the pre-tribulational position is the only viewpoint which can attest to advocating that the return of the Messiah is imminent, meaning that He can return at any moment. But we do not believe that this is a teaching of Scripture; it is rather, an irresponsible interpretation that has been allowed to perpetuate far too long.[45]

25. The exhortation to be comforted by the coming of the Lord (1 Thess. 4:18) is significant only in the pretribulational view, and is especially contradicted by posttribulationism.

This proof claim for pre-tribulationism is an appeal, once again, to the uncontrolled fear of many for the Tribulation period, and their need to be "comforted." Let us examine the reference provided and see whether or not the motives of this line of reasoning are a legitimate support for pre-tribulationism:

"For the Lord Himself will descend from heaven with a shout, with the voice of *the* archangel and with the trumpet of God, and the dead in Messiah will rise first. Then we who are alive and remain will be caught up together with them in the clouds to meet the Lord in the air, and so we shall always be with the Lord. Therefore comfort one another with these words" (1 Thessalonians 4:16-18).

---

[45] Please note that just because one cannot know the exact "day or hour" of Yeshua's return, this does not give any one the license to make rash predictions or unwarranted calculations (or re-calculations) that try to foretell His return, either. It is the proper behavior of the saints that actually hastens His return (2 Peter 3:12).

In these verses, the Apostle Paul does indeed speak of the return of the Messiah and the resurrection of the dead. These are to be encouraging or comforting words for Believers. Notice that Paul's emphasis is on the resurrection; his emphasis is not on any type of "escape." This was largely written to Greeks and Romans, former pagans who had no idea about the resurrection—and may have never even believed in any kind of afterlife at one point—not having the resurrection as a part of their religious upbringing, as their fellow Jewish Believers. So where do pre-tribulationists get the idea that "being comforted" is something that can only be provided by a removal from the Seventieth Week of Israel?

We must first take important notice of the Greek verb variably translated "Console" (NEB), "encourage" (NIV), or "comfort." *Parakaleō* (παρακαλέω) specifically means, "*to call to, exhort, cheer, encourage,*" "*to comfort, console,*" or "*to excite*" (*LS*).[46] Its related noun form is *paraklēsis* (παράκλησις), "*a calling to one's aid, summons,*" "*a calling upon, appealing,*" and "*an exhortation, address*" (*LS*).[47] Noting this, we are now in a proper position to examine whether or not the belief that post-tribulationism does not "comfort" people is valid, or has been misstated.

King David proclaims in Psalm 23:4, "Even though I walk through the valley of the shadow of death, I fear no evil, for You are with me; Your rod and Your staff, they comfort me." The Hebrew verb translated "comfort" is *nacham* (נָחַם), appearing in the Piel stem (intensive action, active voice), meaning "*comfort, console*" (*BDB*).[48] In the Septuagint, *nacham* was rendered as *parakaleō*, indeed indicating that the Lord is able to *comfort* or *encourage* His own while they "walk in the midst of the shadow of death" (LXE). Take notice of the Hebrew word *tzalmavet* (צַלְמָוֶת), which is defined as "**gloom** (deeper than חֹשֶׁךְ [*choshek*]), an impenatrable gloom, pitch, darkness"

---

[46] *LS*, 597.
[47] Ibid.
[48] *BDB*, 637.

(*HALOT*).[49] **Does God have the power to comfort us during any time of tribulation?** Many pre-tribulationists indirectly are saying "No." But we should know better than this. Consider what the Apostle Paul writes in 2 Corinthians 1:3-6:

"Blessed *be* the God and Father of our Lord Yeshua the Messiah, the Father of mercies and God of all comfort, who comforts us in all our affliction so that we will be able to comfort those who are in any affliction [in all our tribulation, KJV][50] with the comfort with which we ourselves are comforted by God. For just as the sufferings of Messiah are ours in abundance, so also our comfort is abundant through Messiah. But if we are afflicted, it is for your comfort and salvation; or if we are comforted, it is for your comfort, which is effective in the patient enduring of the same sufferings which we also suffer."

The answer to the question has to be a resounding "Yes!" because the Lord has the power to comfort us during any kind of difficulty. In fact, Paul writes that He does this so that "we may also be able to comfort (console and encourage) those who are in any kind of trouble or distress" (Amplified Bible). If we are comforted or encouraged by God during any kind of difficulty, be it *general* tribulation or *the* Tribulation, we are to likewise encourage others. This is a far cry from the pre-tribulational position of not being "comforted" because of tribulation. However, as Messianic Believers, the dispensational pre-trib belief suffers even more difficulties when we consider what the Lord comforting His own can often be connected to. Consider what Psalm 119:50-56 says:

"This is my comfort in my affliction, that Your word has revived me. The arrogant utterly deride me, *yet* I do not turn aside from Your law. I have remembered Your ordinances from of old, O LORD, and comfort myself. Burning indignation has seized me because of the

---

[49] *HALOT*, 2:1029.
[50] Grk. *en pasē thlipsei* (ἐν πάσῃ θλίψει).

wicked, who forsake Your law. Your statutes are my songs in the house of my pilgrimage. O LORD, I remember Your name in the night, and keep Your law. This has become mine, that I observe Your precepts."

Notice how the Psalmist is given comfort by the Lord: he heeds God's Instruction and keeps His commandments. Sadly, this is not something that can be said of many contemporary pre-tribulationists, or even post-tribulationists for that same matter, who falsely believe that the Torah or Law of Moses was completely abolished by Yeshua. When one is properly obeying God, one should be able to demonstrate His love and kindness to a world that desperately needs salvation in a very unique and powerful way. How often do even we, as Messianic Believers, forget this?

Now that we understand what true Biblical "comfort" or "encouragement" involves, we can properly interpret Paul's following words in 1 Thessalonians 5:1-4:

"Now as to the times and the epochs, brethren, you have no need of anything to be written to you. For you yourselves know full well that the day of the Lord will come just like a thief in the night. While they are saying, 'Peace and safety!' then destruction will come upon them suddenly like labor pains upon a woman with child, and they will not escape. But you, brethren, are not in darkness, that the day would overtake you like a thief."

Notice that Paul tells the Believers at Thessalonica that the Day of the LORD will come like a thief for those who are not watching and on alert. He tells them that the key for knowing when the Day of the LORD comes is that people will be saying "Peace and safety!" and sudden ruin will come upon them. Is this an indication of any pre-tribulation rapture? When properly understood this is not the case, because the Day of the LORD or *Yom-ADONAI* occurs at the end of the Tribulation period when the *orgē*/wrath of God is poured out on the world.

Believers are to be on guard and on alert so this day does not overtake us. We are to know that this time is nearing when people are exclaiming "Peace and safety!" and believe that things are fine, and they may mock the prophetic message of Scripture (2 Peter 3:4). When this happens terrible things will occur. We are to be comforted and encouraged by the hope of the Messiah's return, the resurrection and transformation of all the saints, and the inauguration of a new era of peace and tranquility on Earth with His direct rule!

26. The exhortation to look for "the glorious appearing" of Christ to His own (Titus 2:13) loses its significance if the tribulation must intervene first. Believers in that case should look for signs.

Titus 2:11-13 says in its entirety, "For the grace of God has appeared, bringing salvation to all men, instructing us to deny ungodliness and worldly desires and to live sensibly, righteously and godly in the present age, looking for the blessed hope and the appearing of the glory of our great God and Savior, Yeshua the Messiah."

The key to properly understanding these verses and whether or not they support a pre-tribulational gathering of the saints, is to properly understand what occurs at the "appearing" (Grk. *epiphaneia*, ἐπιφάνεια) of Yeshua the Messiah. This has already been addressed in detail in *When Will the Messiah Return?* Chapter 2, "The Second Coming," which you should read. It is important that we review the important events that occur at His appearing, because all too often, pre-tribulationists will assert that the Messiah's Second Coming and "appearing" are two separate events. But is this truly the case? I offer the following excerpts from *When Will the Messiah Return?* to restate our ministry position:

> Although Scripture does say that at the Messiah's Second Coming the righteous will be changed "in a twinkling of an eye," it is not a mere "levitation" or a violent snatching away. This is something that Believers are told to "comfort" (NASU) or "encourage" (1 Thessalonians 4:18, NIV) one other with. Those who miss being taken up into the clouds to meet the Lord will suffer a horrible fate. 2 Thessalonians 2:8

specifically speaks of how the antimessiah's rule will be brought to a sudden end by His appearing: "Then that lawless one will be revealed whom the Lord will slay with the breath of His mouth and bring to an end by the appearance of His coming." Even more frightening, though, is how 1 Thessalonians 1:9 says that sinners in general "will pay the penalty of eternal destruction, away from the presence of the Lord and from the glory of His power."

Malachi 4:1-3 emphasizes the physical destruction of the wicked at Yeshua's appearing:

"'For behold, the day is coming, burning like a furnace; and all the arrogant and every evildoer will be chaff; and the day that is coming will set them ablaze,' says the LORD of hosts, 'so that it will leave them neither root nor branch. But for you who fear My name, the sun of righteousness will rise with healing in its wings; and you will go forth and skip about like calves from the stall. You will tread down the wicked, for they will be ashes under the soles of your feet on the day which I am preparing,' says the LORD of hosts."

At the time of the Messiah's appearing in conjunction with the Battle of Armageddon, the antimessiah/antichrist and false prophet will be defeated by Him and immediately thrown into the Lake of Fire (Revelation 19:20), and many others will be physically destroyed (until the second resurrection).[51] Yet in spite of these judgments to be anticipated, Believers who have put their trust in Yeshua, are to eagerly anticipate His *parousia*, as they will meet Him in the clouds, and as Paul so aptly concluded, "so shall we ever be with the Lord" (1 Thessalonians 4:17, KJV).[52]

Knowing this gives us the proper background to understanding whether or not Yeshua's Second Coming and "appearing" are two separate events. As stated further in *When Will the Messiah Return?*,

the term which is most often used in the Apostolic Scriptures as it relates to the Messiah's return is *parousia* (παρουσία), which generally means "coming," "arrival," or "presence." A common pre-tribulational

---

[51] Revelation 20:6, 12-14.
[52] McKee, *WWTMR*, pp 21-22.

tactic is to claim that "the rapture" and Second Coming are separate events. It is often argued that when the Messiah comes for "the Church," He only meets them in the clouds and will only be visible to Believers. It is further thought that when He later comes in the Second Coming, it will only be then that He sets His feet on the Mount of Olives. *But this does not align with the testimony that we see in the Bible concerning His return.* In stark contrast to what pre-tribulationists often argue, the angels testified that He "will come in just the same way[53] as you have watched Him go into heaven" (Acts 1:11)—and surely He was visible to all of those physically present at His ascension. The Lord's ascension was witnessed by more than just the Disciples.[54]

In his book *The Blessed Hope*, author George Eldon Ladd rendered 1 Thessalonians 4:17 with, "We that are alive, that are left unto the parousia of the Lord, shall in no wise precede them that are fallen asleep." In examining the claim that "the rapture" and Second Coming are separate events, Ladd would explain, "It is very difficult to find a secret coming of Christ in [this verse]. His coming will be attended with a shout, with the voice of the archangel, and with the heavenly trumpet."[55]

Ladd similarly renders 2 Thessalonians 2:8: "And then shall be revealed the lawless one, whom the Lord Jesus shall slay with the breath of his mouth, and bring to naught by the manifestation of his parousia." He comments, "This [coming] is obviously no secret event, for the parousia of Christ will be an outshining, a manifestation....[T]his verse locates the parousia at the end of the Tribulation. One would naturally conclude by comparing the verses just cited that the Rapture of the living saints, the resurrection of those who have died, and the judgment upon the Antichrist will all take place

---

[53] Grk. *hon tropon* (ὃν τρόπον), "in what manner" (YLT).
[54] McKee, *WWTMR*, pp 24-25.
[55] Ladd, 63.

at the same time, namely, at the parousia of Jesus at the end of the Tribulation."[56]

It is important for us to note that Paul told the Thessalonicans to "establish your hearts without blame in holiness before our God and Father at the coming of our Lord Yeshua with all His saints" (1 Thessalonians 3:13). Contrary to what some pre-tribulationists may argue, this is actually a support for a post-tribulational gathering of the elect. Some have used this verse as a proof for pre-tribulationism arguing that the "saints" mentioned here are those who have been raptured into Heaven prior to the Tribulation period. But the "holy ones" (NIV) are primarily the disembodied consciousnesses of born again Believers which are coming with the Messiah to be reunited with their resurrected physical bodies at His *parousia*. They are not people who were supposedly "taken up" in the rapture to Heaven prior to the Tribulation period. If a pre-tribulation rapture were implied here, then Paul would not have admonished Believers to establish their hearts before God until the Messiah's *parousia* or "arrival" to claim His Earthly throne and defeat His enemies.

Furthermore, in 2 Thessalonians 2:1, Paul speaks of "the coming of our Lord Jesus Christ and our being gathered to him" (NIV). The Greek is even more specific, reading *tēs parousias tou Kuriou hēmōn Iēsou Christou kai hēmōn episunagōgēs ep' auton* (τῆς παρουσίας τοῦ κυρίου ἡμῶν Ἰησοῦ Χριστοῦ καὶ ἡμῶν ἐπισυναγωγῆς ἐπ' αὐτὸν). This indicates that Yeshua's **coming** and **gathering** of the saints are indeed *the same event*, and cannot be separated. The Greek text is quite clear on this point.[57]

The Messiah's appearing and Second Coming are part of the same event; they are not separated. Paul admonishes Titus and the Believers he must care for that Messiah followers are to live holy and righteous lives and look forward to Yeshua's appearing. At His appearing, Yeshua will defeat the antimessiah and bring his rule to

---

[56] Ibid.
[57] McKee, *WWTMR*, pp 25-26.

an end. Of course, a critical issue remaining is how we are supposed to live holy lives. Paul tells us in Titus 2:14 that Yeshua "gave Himself for us to redeem us from every lawless deed, and to purify for Himself a people for His own possession, zealous for good deeds." Or, "He gave himself up on our behalf in order to free us from all violation of *Torah*" (CJB). In order to properly look forward to the return of the Messiah and His appearing, we must be free from all lawlessness and be in diligent obedience to our Heavenly Father (Exodus 19:5; Deuteronomy 4:20). How often do we see this emphasized by pre-tribulationists? Probably not enough.

27. The exhortation to purify ourselves in view of the Lord's return has most significance if His coming is imminent (1 John 3:2-3).

1 John 3:2-3 says in its entirety, "Beloved, now we are children of God, and it has not appeared as yet what we will be. We know that when He appears, we will be like Him, because we will see Him just as He is. And everyone who has this hope *fixed* on Him purifies himself, just as He is pure."

The admonition to be purified from sin is extremely important, especially in light of the Messiah's return and the gathering of the saints. Whether you are a pre-tribulationist or post-tribulationist, you should believe this to be true because of the sin that will be prevailing in intensity as Yeshua's return draws nearer. One day, we will all be changed and have a restored body similar to the one He has (cf. Philippians 3:21). But does this necessarily indicate that the Messiah's return can happen at any moment? Are Christians today seeking to purify themselves of sin as the Apostle John tells us to? Pre-tribulationists need to be very careful when referencing these verses as a supposed proof of pre-tribulationism. The Apostle John states the following in regard to knowing Yeshua and following His example:

"And everyone who has this hope *fixed* on Him purifies himself, just as He is pure. Everyone who practices sin also practices lawlessness; and sin is lawlessness. You know that He appeared in order to take away sins; and in Him there is no sin. No one who abides in Him sins; no one who sins has seen Him or knows Him" (1 John 3:3-6).

If we know Yeshua as our Lord and Savior and believe that He is God, then we will follow His commandments—the commandments delivered by Him in the Torah or Law of Moses. We will walk as Yeshua walked, living the Torah as He followed it, and demonstrating appropriate actions. This is something that many pre-tribulationists do not do or fully understand.

We are to purify ourselves and rid ourselves of sin by not disobeying God's commandments, because John follows up his words on purifying ourselves with the ever-critical, "Everyone who practices sin also practices lawlessness; and sin is lawlessness" (1 John 3:4). Furthermore, if we discipline ourselves to study the Torah, we see that the need for us to be a holy and set-apart people is self-apparent. In relation to the Last Days it is imperative that we be separated from the world, and especially remember that the Tribulation saints "keep the commandments of God and hold to the testimony of Yeshua" (Revelation 12:17).

This is not a proof for pre-tribulationism; it is rather a proof for God's people to purify themselves by ceding more control of their lives over to Him by obeying Him. **This is something that is extremely important if Believers are to be separate from the world and endure the end-times!**

28. The church is uniformly exhorted to look for the coming of the Lord, whereas believers in the tribulation are directed to look for signs.

We agree with the pre-tribulationists here that Believers who compose the *ekklēsia* are to look for the coming of the Lord, but the coming of the Lord here is falsely believed to occur as the pre-tribulation rapture. As already mentioned, the Greek word often translated as "coming" in reference to the coming of Yeshua is *parousia* (παρουσία), which *Vine* describes as "lit., 'a presence,' *para* [παρά], 'with,' and *ousia* [οὐσία], 'being' (from *eimi* [εἰμί], 'to be'), denotes both an 'arrival' and a consequent 'presence with.'"[58] Just looking at this definition, does it imply any pre-tribulation rapture? No, it does not. It does not, because the idea being conveyed is that the Messiah comes and He reveals His presence.

Let us now examine where *parousia* is used so we can have a proper understanding of the Lord's coming and why it is not pre-tribulational. The Disciples asked Yeshua about His *parousia* in Matthew 24:3:

"As He was sitting on the Mount of Olives, the disciples came to Him privately, saying, 'Tell us, when will these things happen, and what *will* be the sign of Your coming [*parousia*], and of the end of the age?'"

Yeshua answered them with the critical words, "For just as the lightning comes from the east and flashes even to the west, so will the coming [*parousia*] of the Son of Man be" (Matthew 24:27). The Lord also told them, "Wherever the corpse is, there the vultures will gather" (Matthew 24:28), emphasizing that this would something attendant to look for at *His Coming*. It is after this admonition, not surprisingly, that He says He will gather the saints "after the tribulation of those days" (Matthew 24:29-31). Further information about what occurs at His Coming or *parousia* is given in Matthew 24:37-39:

---

[58] *Vine*, 111.

"For the coming [*parousia*] of the Son of Man will be just like the days of Noah. For as in those days before the flood they were eating and drinking, marrying and giving in marriage, until the day that Noah entered the ark, and they did not understand until the flood came and took them all away; so will the coming of the Son of Man be." Notice what happens at the Messiah's *parousia:* **there is not a secret gathering of the saints.** Paul compliments this with saying in 2 Thessalonians 2:8, "that [the] lawless one will be revealed whom the Lord will slay with the breath of His mouth and bring to an end by the appearance of His coming [*parousia*]." The Messiah will defeat the antimessiah/antichrist at His *parousia*, which the pre-tribulationists are telling us is pre-tribulational, yet the *parousia* here is clearly placed in a post-tribulational context. This mirrors Revelation 19:20:

"And the beast was seized, and with him the false prophet who performed the signs in his presence, by which he deceived those who had received the mark of the beast and those who worshiped his image; these two were thrown alive into the lake of fire which burns with brimstone."

Again, does this imply a pre-tribulational return of Yeshua? No. It speaks of the Day of the LORD or *Yom-ADONAI* and His judgment upon Planet Earth.

Are we to look for the coming of the Lord? Yes. But we are also to be on guard and on alert. The ultimate end of the Tribulation period is not the rise of the New World Order or the antimessiah/antichrist; it is the coming of Yeshua the Messiah and the establishment of His Kingdom. But clearly from the passages that we have addressed which speak of His *parousia*, His coming is post-tribulational. Paul admonishes Believers in 1 Thessalonians 3:13 that Yeshua "may establish your hearts without blame in holiness before our God and Father at the coming [*parousia*] of our Lord Yeshua with all His saints." Interestingly enough, those of us who are Messianic should know what holiness fully involves: being set-apart unto the Lord by keeping His commandments. This is something that we have to do if we intend to be blameless and ready at the *parousia* of Yeshua.

THE WORK OF THE HOLY SPIRIT?

29. The Holy Spirit as the Restrainer of evil cannot be taken out of the world unless the church, which the Spirit indwells, is translated at the same time. The tribulation cannot begin until this restraint is lifted.

This claim has already been addressed previously, and we have discussed how we do not believe that the Holy Spirit is the restrainer, but rather that it is the Archangel Michael (2 Thessalonians 2:6; cf. Daniel 12:1; Revelation 12:7). The next proof given for pre-tribulationism is more specific than this one, so we will address and review our points for both #29 and #30 at the same time under #30.

30. The Holy Spirit as the Restrainer must be taken out of the world before "the lawless one," who dominates the tribulation period, can be revealed (2 Thess. 2:6-8).

2 Thessalonians 2:6-8 says in its entirety, "And you know what restrains him now, so that in his time he will be revealed. For the mystery of lawlessness is already at work; only he who now restrains *will do so* until he is taken out of the way. Then that lawless one will be revealed whom the Lord will slay with the breath of His mouth and bring to an end by the appearance of His coming." These verses do not explicitly identify the Holy Spirit as the restraining force which presently holds back the man of lawlessness from coming on the scene. The New King James Version, for example, actually capitalizes the "He," implying that it is Divine and part of

the Godhead, yet this is a theological value judgment which has been made by its publishers.

The idea promoted by pre-tribulationists is that "the Church," which is indwelt by the Holy Spirit, must be removed for the antimessiah/antichrist to be revealed. Yet at the same time pre-tribulationists will also argue that there will be multitudes upon multitudes of Tribulation saints. If the Holy Spirit is removed as they claim, then there can be no Tribulation saints, because **true Believers must be regenerated by the Holy Spirit.** But then there are other pre-tribulationists who say that this restraint of the Holy Spirit being removed is only temporary, and that the Holy Spirit will return once "the Church" has been raptured to Heaven. Where is the basis for this in Scripture? The simple truth of the matter is that there is none. Its basis is in escapism.

The belief, that the Archangel Michael is really the restrainer, has its basis in Scripture. Consider Daniel 12:1: "Now at that time Michael, the great prince who stands *guard* over the sons of your people, will arise. And there will be a time of distress such as never occurred since there was a nation until that time; and at that time your people, everyone who is found written in the book, will be rescued." Compare this to Revelation 12:7-9 and the prophesied war in Heaven:

"And there was war in heaven, Michael and his angels waging war with the dragon. The dragon and his angels waged war, and they were not strong enough, and there was no longer a place found for them in heaven. And the great dragon was thrown down, the serpent of old who is called the devil and Satan, who deceives the whole world; he was thrown down to the earth, and his angels were thrown down with him."

Daniel 12:1 states that Michael "will arise" (NIV). The verb used is *amad* (עָמַד), "meaning to stand, to rise up; to take one's stand" (*AMG*).[59] Daniel 12:1 is a reference to the war in Heaven in Revelation 12, and Michael and his

---

[59] Warren Baker and Eugene Carpenter, eds., *Complete Word Study Dictionary: Old Testament* (Chattanooga: AMG Publishing, 2003), 843.

forces casting Satan down to the Earth. The Archangel Michael is the one who is presently restraining the full force of evil, but one day that restraint will be lifted and Satan will be able to have full reign for 42 months. Notice what Revelation 12:10-12 tells us:

"Then I heard a loud voice in heaven, saying, 'Now the salvation, and the power, and the kingdom of our God and the authority of His Messiah have come, for the accuser of our brethren has been thrown down, he who accuses them before our God day and night. And they overcame him because of the blood of the Lamb and because of the word of their testimony, and they did not love their life even when faced with death. For this reason, rejoice, O heavens and you who dwell in them. Woe to the earth and the sea, because the devil has come down to you, having great wrath, knowing that he has *only* a short time.'"

When the restraint on evil will be lifted, the enemy will have only a short season. The Holy Spirit is not the restrainer, because pre-tribulationists cannot offer any verses to substantiate it. But we have offered proof texts from Daniel 12 and Revelation 12 that directly compliment Paul's admonition in 2 Thessalonians. After Michael takes his stand in Heaven, there "will be a time of trouble, the like of which has never been since the nation came into being. At that time, your people will be rescued, all who are found inscribed in the book" (Daniel 12:1b, NJPS). The Hebrew word for "distress" is *tzarah* (צָרָה), whose Septuagint equivalent is *thlipsis* (θλῖψις), the same term used in the Apostolic Scriptures for "tribulation." This also mirrors Yeshua's words, "For then there will be a great tribulation, such as has not occurred since the beginning of the world until now, nor ever will" (Matthew 24:21). Interestingly enough, when this takes place Revelation 12:11 says that the saints overcome the power and influence of the Adversary—hardly an inference of a pre-tribulation rapture escape.

So what is the basis for believing that the Holy Spirit is the restrainer? There is none.

31. If the expression, "except the falling away come first," be translated literally, "except the departure come first," it would plainly show the necessity of the rapture taking place before the beginning of the tribulation.

We have already addressed this reason, but it is important that we review it again. This proof is commonly based on 2 Thessalonians 2:3. We quote it from the KJV, which uses "falling away":

"Let no man deceive you by any means: for *that day shall not come*, except there come **a falling away first,**[60] and that man of sin be revealed, the son of perdition."

Many pre-tribulationists believe that the "falling away" is in actuality the "rapture of the Church." Their problem is that the Greek text does not substantiate this belief at all. The Greek word rendered as "falling away" in the KJV is *apostasia* (ἀποστασία). The RSV and NIV render this as "rebellion," and the NASU and HCSB translate it as "apostasy." When considering the fact that many modern Bibles are produced by pre-tribulationists, if "departure" were a valid translation, then why is it not used in these versions?

The only other location that *apostasia* is used in the Apostolic Scriptures is in Acts 21:21 where Paul is falsely accused of teaching the Jewish Believers to abandon the Torah:

"[A]nd they have been told about you, that you are teaching all the Jews who are among the Gentiles to forsake [*apostasia*] Moses,[61] telling them not to circumcise their children nor to walk according to the customs" (Acts 21:21).

The NIV renders this as "turn away from Moses," and HCSB has "abandon Moses." So, if the "forsaking" or "turning away" or "abandoning" must occur before the return of Yeshua, where is the implication of any pre-tribulation rapture? The logic behind making the

---

[60] Grk. *hē apostasia prōton* (ἡ ἀποστασία πρῶτον).

[61] Grk. *hoti apostasian didaskeis apo Mōseōs* (ὅτι ἀποστασίαν διδάσκεις ἀπὸ Μωϋσέως), "that apostasy from Moses thou dost teach" (YLT).

"apostasy" a good thing or a "departure" is mind-boggling. Why is this perhaps the case? It might just be because pre-tribulationists are unwilling to accept the reality that much of contemporary Christianity, sadly, steadily edging further toward apostasy, and abandoning the foundational truths of Scripture. With the rise of the Messianic movement and the emphasis that we place on Believers living the Torah obedient life of Yeshua, such apostasy is, unfortunately, becoming easier for us to identify.[62] It is fitting that the only other place that *apostasia* is mentioned outside of 2 Thessalonians 2:3 is Acts 21:21. Be encouraged by the verses which precede it:

"After we arrived in Jerusalem, the brethren received us gladly. And the following day Paul went in with us to James, and all the elders were present. After he had greeted them, he *began* to relate one by one the things which God had done among the Gentiles through his ministry. And when they heard it they *began* glorifying God; and they said to him, 'You see, brother, how many thousands there are among the Jews of those who have believed, and they are all zealous for the Law'" (Acts 21:17-20).

This speaks of the many "myriads" (YLT) of First Century Jewish Believers in Messiah Yeshua who continued to follow the Torah after their conversion of faith. In the future there will be myriads of Tribulation saints, *both Jews and non-Jews*, who also know Messiah Yeshua and are likewise zealous to obey God (cf. Revelation 12:17; 14:12).

---

[62] For a further examination of this issue, consult Chapter 7 in *When Will the Messiah Return?*: "The Great Apostasy."

NECESSITY OF AN INTERVAL BETWEEN THE RAPTURE AND THE SECOND COMING?

32. According to 2 Corinthians 5:10, all believers of this age must appear before the judgment seat of Christ in heaven, an event never mentioned in the detailed accounts connected with the second coming of Christ to the earth.

It is correct to assert that all Believers will appear before the judgment, or *bēma* (βῆμα) seat, of the Messiah. This is clearly stated in 2 Corinthians 5:10: "For we must all appear before the judgment seat of Messiah, so that each one may be recompensed for his deeds in the body, according to what he has done, whether good or bad." But the context of this wider passage, 2 Corinthians 5:1-10, does not speak of any pre-tribulation rapture. This is largely a discussion about Paul's preference of never dying, and instead "longing to be clothed with our dwelling from heaven" (2 Corinthians 5:2), meaning his being over-clothed with an immortal body at the time of the Messiah's return. The reality for most people, though, is that while it may never be their wish to die (2 Corinthians 5:3-4), is that they will die. And so, Paul acknowledges how "to be absent from the body and [is] to be at home with the Lord" (2 Corinthians 5:8). Death as a Believer, while it may mean a condition of disembodiment—means existence in the presence of the Messiah in Heaven (cf. Philippians 1:23)!

What is difficult for some modern Christian readers to compute, is why if preference is given to a bodiless state in the Lord's presence—Paul must remind the Ancient Corinthians, "Therefore we also have as our ambition, whether at home or absent, to be pleasing to Him. For we must all appear before the judgment seat of Messiah, so that each one may be recompensed for his deeds in the body, according to what he has done, whether good or bad" (2 Corinthians 5:9-10). Obviously, regardless of what happens in our lives on Planet Earth, the righteous are to be pleasing to God in their conduct. The challenge is that for many ancient Greeks and Romans, who were not reared in a religious environment where a future resurrection was stressed—is that they might have believed that a bodiless condition was to be so preferred, that physical actions in daily human living were not that important. Paul's view of a temporary, disembodied afterlife in Heaven, has no room for such a thought. All of the Messiah's followers, whether they find themselves as having been at home in the body *or* absent from the body at one point, will appear before Him for an evaluation of their good works.

The claim that the specific rewards to be issued before the righteous, do not occur in relation to the Second Coming, is without any substantial basis. Isaiah 40:10 tells us, "Behold, the Lord GOD will come with might, with His arm ruling for Him. Behold, His reward is with Him and His recompense before Him." Isaiah 62:11 also says, "Behold, the LORD has proclaimed to the end of the earth, say to the daughter of Zion, 'Lo, your salvation comes; behold His reward is with Him, and His recompense before Him.'" Both of these verses tell us that when Yeshua the Messiah returns "his reward is with him, and his recompense accompanies him" (NIV). Standing before the *bēma* seat of Messiah is to be likened to the end of a race where one is congratulated by an official (cf. 2 Timothy 4:7; Hebrews 12:1-2)—the race of life that is hard run by the faithful who trust in Yeshua. The rewards are issued to God's people—both the deceased-resurrected and living—subsequent to the Second Coming, on Earth. This is why Paul was able to tell the Thessalonicans, "For who is our hope or joy or crown of exultation? Is it not even you, in the presence of our Lord Yeshua at His coming? For you are our glory and joy" (1 Thessalonians 2:19-20). All of the righteous saints get to stand before the *bēma* together (cf. 1 Thessalonians 4:17), as the Millennium begins, and they are specifically rewarded for their faithfulness (cf. 2 Timothy 4:8).

33. If the twenty-four elders of Revelation 4:1-5:14 are representative of the church, as many expositors believe, it would necessitate the rapture and reward of the church before the tribulation.

As Messianic post-tribulationists, we do not believe, as do pre-tribulationists, that the twenty-four elders represent the "raptured Church." Walvoord has done well with prefacing his remarks with the conditional "If..." The Apostle John is told in Revelation 4:1, "After these things I looked, and behold, a door *standing* open in heaven, and the first voice which I had heard, like *the sound* of a trumpet speaking with me, said, 'Come up here, and I will show you what must take place after these things.'" John is the one who is told to come into Heaven, not "the Church" as is commonly believed. John is shown things that, as far as the elders are concerned, have already occurred.

It does not make sense at all that the twenty-four elders would comprise "the Church," as it is called, but rather the Twelve Tribes of Israel and the Twelve Apostles. This is especially true given the tone and symbolism of the Book of Revelation. Consider Revelation 21:12, 14: "It had a great and high wall, with twelve gates, and at the gates twelve angels; and names *were* written on them, which are *the names* of the twelve tribes of the sons of Israel...And the wall of the city had twelve foundation stones, and on them *were* the twelve names of the twelve apostles of the Lamb." This is describing the city of New Jerusalem.

Walvoord's key argument here is "If the twenty-four elders...are representative of the church." This does not appear to be the case. In fact, one might say the twelve foundations with the names of the Apostles of New Jerusalem is about as "churchy," so to speak, as the Eternal State gets. The twenty-four elders actually represent a restored Israel.

34. The coming of Christ for His bride must take place before the second coming to the earth for the wedding feast (Rev. 19:7-10).

It is interesting that Revelation 19 is referenced for support of the marriage of the Messiah to His Bride, when this chapter occurs *at the end* of the Book of Revelation—not at the beginning. While there is debate over the sequencing of the judgments of the Tribulation, insomuch that prophecy teachers are divided over whether or not the seals, trumpets, and vials/bowls occur one at a time *or* rather in a "symphony" of judgments, it is mostly agreed among pre-millennialists that the events at the end of Revelation occur at the end of the Great Tribulation and then carry over to the Millennial Kingdom and into the Eternal State. Let us now review the verses in question and place them into their correct context:

"'Let us rejoice and be glad and give the glory to Him, for the marriage of the Lamb has come and His bride has made herself ready.' It was given to her to clothe herself in fine linen, bright *and* clean; for the fine linen is the righteous acts of the saints. Then he said to me, 'Write, "Blessed are those who are invited to the marriage supper of the Lamb."' And he said to me, 'These are true words of God.' Then I fell at his feet to worship him. But he said to me, 'Do not do that; I am a fellow servant of yours and your brethren who hold the testimony of Yeshua; worship God. For the testimony of Yeshua is the spirit of prophecy'" (Revelation 19:7-10).

These verses do speak of a future Marriage Supper of the Lamb and marriage of Messiah Yeshua to Believers— at least of an *allegorical marriage* where we as Believers should presently be chaste and virtuous awaiting their coming husband. But do the events in Revelation 19, as claimed by Walvoord, occur in a pre-tribulational context? Not at all. Revelation 19:9 first tells us, "Blessed are those who are invited to the marriage supper of the Lamb." After this, John immediately records the words, "I saw heaven opened, and behold, a white horse, and He who sat on it *is* called Faithful and True, and in righteousness He judges and wages war" (Revelation 19:11). This describes the appearing of the Messiah; but it is not the pre-tribulation rapture. Revelation 19:11 tells us that Yeshua sits on a white horse and that "With justice he judges and makes war" (NIV).

If you continue reading Revelation 19:12-21, you will see that the context of Yeshua appearing, and thus the Marriage Supper of the Lamb occurring, is very clearly post-tribulational. The Messiah appears and defeats His enemies *first*, including casting the antimessiah/antichrist and the false prophet into the Lake of Fire:

> "His eyes *are* a flame of fire, and on His head *are* many diadems; and He has a name written *on Him* which no one knows except Himself. *He is* clothed with a robe dipped in blood, and His name is called The Word of God. And the armies which are in heaven, clothed in fine linen, white *and* clean, were following Him on white horses. From His mouth comes a sharp sword, so that with it He may strike down the nations, and He will rule them with a rod of iron; and He treads the wine press of the fierce wrath of God, the Almighty. And on His robe and on His thigh He has a name written, 'KING OF KINGS, AND LORD OF LORDS.' Then I saw an angel standing in the sun, and he cried out with a loud voice, saying to all the birds which fly in midheaven, 'Come, assemble for the great supper of God, so that you may eat the flesh of kings and the flesh of commanders and the flesh of mighty men and the flesh of horses and of those who sit on them and the flesh of all men, both free men and slaves, and small and great.' And I saw the beast and the kings of the earth and their armies assembled to make war against Him who sat on the horse and against His army. And the beast was seized, and with him the false prophet who performed the signs in his presence, by which he deceived those who had received the mark of the beast and those who worshiped his image; these two were thrown alive into the lake of fire which burns with brimstone. And the rest were killed with the sword which came from the mouth of Him who sat on the horse, and all the birds were filled with their flesh."

The Scriptures do tell us that there will be a Marriage Supper of the Lamb. The problem for pre-tribulationists is that when this takes place, it is when the Lord returns to defeat His enemies *at the end of the Tribulation*. In Revelation 19:7-21 there is both an invitation and a warning: Join the Marriage Supper of the Lamb *or* be judged when the Lamb returns in vengeance to defeat His enemies. If you will not be a part of the Marriage Supper when He returns, then prepare to be a recipient of His wrath.

35. Tribulation saints are not translated at the second coming of Christ but carry on ordinary occupations such as farming and building houses, and shall bear children (Isa. 65:20-25). This would be impossible if all saints were translated at the second coming to the earth as posttribulationists teach.

This proof for pre-tribulationism claims that if all saints are translated and transformed in a post-tribulational context at the Second Coming, then it would be impossible for people to live normal lives during the Millennial Kingdom and bear children. Is it completely impossible, or is this simply a requirement imposed by pre-tribulationists? Is it required for there to be a pre-tribulation rapture so that there is procreation during the Millennium? Consider Isaiah's prophecy of the coming Millennial Kingdom, where there will clearly be reproduction of humans:

"No longer will there be in it an infant *who lives but a few* days, or an old man who does not live out his days; for the youth will die at the age of one hundred and the one who does not reach the age of one hundred will be *thought* accursed. They will build houses and inhabit *them*; they will also plant vineyards and eat their fruit. They will not build and another inhabit, they will not plant and another eat; for as the lifetime of a tree, *so will be* the days of My people, and My chosen ones will wear out the work of their hands. They will not labor in vain, or bear *children* for calamity; for they are the offspring of those blessed by the LORD, and their descendants with them. It will also come to pass that before they call, I will answer; and while they are still speaking, I will hear. The wolf and the lamb will graze together, and the lion will eat straw like the ox; and dust will be the serpent's food. They will do no evil or harm in all My holy mountain,' says the LORD" (Isaiah 65:20-25).

This passage referenced by Walvoord from the Tanach (Old Testament) testifies of the lifestyle of those during the Millennium. There will be those who live and die. Notably, the *ArtScroll Tanach* comments that "People will have such longevity that dying at the age of one hundred will be considered as dying young, or it will be considered as a punishment to die at that age."[63] This might indicate that dying is a punishment for sin, as during this period the Messiah will be ruling and reigning over the Earth, and this may be for capital offenses, or perhaps more likely offenses directly associated with apostasy and blasphemy against the King. We may not know for sure until this takes place. Nevertheless, a pre-tribulation rapture is not required so that there will be those who can procreate.

The Apostle Paul writes in 1 Corinthians 15:51, "Behold, I tell you a mystery; we will not all sleep, but we will all be changed." What he says is that *not all the saints will die*, but that all the saints will be transformed. The Greek verb *allassō* (ἀλλάσσω) can mean *"to make other than it is, to change, alter,"* or *"to interchange, alternate"* (*LS*).[64] The mystery that Paul speaks of here is that all are going to be translated, but not all Believers are going to have their bodies die. What of those who do not die? Is it possible that these people receive redeemed bodies similar to Adam and Eve's prior to the Fall, and thus are responsible for repopulating the Earth at the start of the

---

[63] Nosson Scherman and Meir Zlotowitz, eds., *ArtScroll Tanach* (Brooklyn: Mesorah Publications, Ltd., 1996), 1065.
[64] *LS*, 37.

Millennium? This is something that most pre-tribulationists I have encountered do not have an answer for.

Some may, however, use Yeshua's words in Matthew 22:30 to rebuff the idea that translated saints who never die procreate during the Millennium. He says, "in the resurrection they neither marry nor are given in marriage, but are like angels in heaven." This is most certainly true of the saints who die in the faith and whose bodies are resurrected at the Messiah's appearing. But again, what of those who are changed and do not die? Some Believers will *never* have to be resurrected.

It is not necessary for there to be a pre-tribulation rapture of the saints to leave "non-translated" saints on Earth when Yeshua returns to rule and reign. We are clearly told that all will be changed, but that not all will die. It is possible that those who never die, but are changed, are those who are largely responsible for repopulating the Earth during the Millennium, similar to how Adam and Eve were intended to populate the Earth in the Garden of Eden (Genesis 1:28).

36. The judgment of the Gentiles following the second coming (Matt. 25:31-46) indicates that both saved and unsaved are still in their natural bodies, which would be impossible if the translation had taken place at the second coming.

Upon the initial reading of this reason, many will accept these claims at face value and never examine Matthew 25 and consider what the exact context is of the passage where the nations are separated. The claim being made here is that the nations are separated out at the beginning of the Millennium, just following Yeshua's *parousia* or Second Coming. Because "the rapture" and Second Coming are believed to be separate events, only those who are determined to be "saved" can enter into the Millennial Kingdom. However, a close review of

Matthew 25:31-46 does not reveal this to be the case. We need to place this passage into its appropriate setting:

"But when the Son of Man comes in His glory, and all the angels with Him, then He will sit on His glorious throne. All the nations will be gathered before Him; and He will separate them from one another, as the shepherd separates the sheep from the goats; and He will put the sheep on His right, and the goats on the left. Then the King will say to those on His right, 'Come, you who are blessed of My Father, inherit the kingdom prepared for you from the foundation of the world'" (Matthew 25:31-34).

Yeshua the Messiah says that He will come in glory and sit on His throne. Walvoord's assertion is that the nations are gathered before Yeshua at the start of the Millennium, and the sheep are separated from the goats, the sheep supposedly being those who are saved during the Tribulation, being found worthy to enter into the Kingdom. While the sheep are allowed to enter into the Kingdom, *what Kingdom* is being talked about here? Is it the Millennial Kingdom? Consider what the Lord says next:

"'For I was hungry, and you gave Me *something* to eat; I was thirsty, and you gave Me *something* to drink; I was a stranger, and you invited Me in; naked, and you clothed Me; I was sick, and you visited Me; I was in prison, and you came to Me.' Then the righteous will answer Him, 'Lord, when did we see You hungry, and feed You, or thirsty, and give You *something* to drink? And when did we see You a stranger, and invite You in, or naked, and clothe You? When did we see You sick, or in prison, and come to You?' The King will answer and say to them, 'Truly I say to you, to the extent that you did it to one of these brothers of Mine, *even* the least *of them*, you did it to Me'" (Matthew 25:35-40).

Yeshua the Messiah gives a list of things as to how people should have been ministering to one another (cf. 1 John 3:14-15). This is instruction which surely applies to *more* than just those who experienced the Tribulation, but to people of all times who encountered Yeshua's teachings, and then responded to them with either obedience or disobedience. Some of these are those who enter into God's Kingdom, and they are prompted to ask the Lord why they are regarded as righteous. They followed the proper example of all of Scripture and cared for and served others. Notice what Yeshua then says:

"Then He will also say to those on His left, 'Depart from Me, accursed ones, into the eternal fire which has been prepared for the devil and his angels; for I was hungry, and you gave Me *nothing* to eat; I was thirsty, and you gave Me nothing to drink; I was a stranger, and you did not invite Me in; naked, and you did not clothe Me; sick, and in prison, and you did not visit Me.' Then they themselves also will answer, 'Lord, when did we see You hungry, or thirsty, or a stranger, or naked, or sick, or in prison, and did not take care of You?' Then He will answer them, 'Truly I say to you, to the extent that you did not do it to one of the least of these, you did not do it to Me'" (Matthew 25:41-45).

Those who fail to serve and care are told, "The curse is upon you; go from my sight into the eternal fire that is ready for the devil and his angels" (NEB). They are not only not allowed to enter into the Kingdom, but they are thrown into the Lake of Fire. This gives us a clue as to *when* this separation occurs. Matthew 25:46 further indicates, "These will go away into eternal punishment, but the righteous into eternal life." The Kingdom which is being referenced here at the separation of the nations, the sheep from the goats—"the kingdom prepared for you from the foundation of the world" (Matthew 25:34)—is very clearly the Eternal Kingdom of God in the redeemed state which arrives following the end of the Millennium. The throne referenced in Matthew 25:31 is the Great White Throne of Yeshua the Messiah (Revelation 20:11). It is obvious from the text that those who do not enter this Kingdom are thrown into eternal punishment and everlasting separation from God.

When placed in its appropriate context, the separation of the sheep from the goats is not a support for pre-tribulationism. This does not occur at the start of the

Millennial Kingdom, but rather following the end of the Millennium when those who do not enter into the Eternal Kingdom of the Lord suffer the penalty of eternal punishment.[65]

37. If the translation took place in connection with the second coming to the earth, there would be no need of separating the sheep from the goats at the subsequent judgment, but the separation would have taken place in the very act of the translation of the believers before Christ actually sets up His throne on earth (Matt. 25:31).

This is not entirely true as we have just discussed. The separation of the sheep and the goats occurs following the end of the Millennium. The sheep enter into the Eternal Kingdom of God and the goats are cast into the Lake of Fire.

THE RAPTURE AND THE SECOND COMING CONTRASTS BETWEEN?

38. The judgment of Israel (Ezek. 20:34-38) which occurs subsequent to the second coming indicates the necessity of regathering Israel. The separation of the saved from the unsaved in this judgment obviously takes place sometime after the second coming and would be unnecessary if the saved had previously been separated from the unsaved by translation.

What is the context of Ezekiel 20:34-38 referenced in regard to the judgment of Israel?
"'I will bring you out from the peoples and gather you from the lands where you are scattered, with a mighty

---

[65] For a further discussion, consult the author's publication *Why Hell Must Be Eternal*.

hand and with an outstretched arm and with wrath poured out; and I will bring you into the wilderness of the peoples, and there I will enter into judgment with you face to face. As I entered into judgment with your fathers in the wilderness of the land of Egypt, so I will enter into judgment with you,' declares the Lord GOD. 'I will make you pass under the rod, and I will bring you into the bond of the covenant; and I will purge from you the rebels and those who transgress against Me; I will bring them out of the land where they sojourn, but they will not enter the land of Israel. Thus you will know that I am the LORD.'"

The Scriptures are quite clear that there will be an end-time regathering and restoration of Israel, meaning the physical descendants of Abraham, Isaac, and Jacob, to the Holy Land prior to the return of the Messiah. The difference between the pre-tribulationists and Messianic post-tribulationists like ourselves, is that we believe that we are a part of the community of Israel and not a part of some separate "Church." We believe that if we enter into the Tribulation period in our lifetimes, that we will be there to somehow be a part of this event. While non-Jewish Believers should not expect an inheritance in the Holy Land when Yeshua returns, they are nonetheless to be regarded as a part of Israel's polity and Kingdom realm.

Contrary to what is attested, the separation of the saved from the unsaved, or righteous from the unrighteous, in this judgment does not occur after the Second Coming. The Lord says that He will take His people into the wilderness, "and I will contend with you there, face to face" (ATS). Just as during the Exodus the Lord took His people out of Egypt and then divided those who would enter into the Promised Land, and those who would not, during the 40 years in the wilderness, so will it be during the Tribulation period. The unrighteous will be separated out in this future wilderness experience, so the righteous will be all who are left when the Messiah returns.

A sad lack of understanding this Biblical reality is apparent here, because pre-tribulationists fail to see themselves as a part of Israel and understand the patterns of the Torah.

39. At the time of the rapture the saints meet Christ in the air, while at the second coming Christ returns to the Mount of Olives to meet the saints on earth.

As discussed in *When Will the Messiah Return?* and detailed further on, the correct context of the "meeting" of Believers with the Messiah in the air (1 Thessalonians 4:17), is that the saints will meet Him and then *we will all* return to Earth together. This will occur just as the Believers in Rome met Paul at Three Taverns (or Three Inns), and then all of them entered into the city of Rome together (Acts 28:16). Similarly, when Yeshua returns, the saints will meet Him in the air, and then turn around as the judgments of God are poured out on Planet Earth and the Battle of Armageddon ensues. I believe that this is the correct interpretation regarding Yeshua's return to the Mount of Olives as detailed in Zechariah 14:

> "Behold, a day is coming for the LORD when the spoil taken from you will be divided among you. For I will gather all the nations against Jerusalem to battle, and the city will be captured, the houses plundered, the women ravished and half of the city exiled, but the rest of the people will not be cut off from the city. Then the LORD will go forth and fight against those nations, as when He fights on a day of battle. In that day His feet will stand on the Mount of Olives, which is in front of Jerusalem on the east; and the Mount of Olives will be split in its middle from east to west by a very large valley, so that half of the mountain will move toward the north and the other half toward the south...Now this will be the plague with which the LORD will strike all the peoples who have gone to war against Jerusalem; their flesh will rot while they stand on their feet, and their eyes will rot in their sockets, and their tongue will rot in their mouth. It will come about in that day that a

great panic from the LORD will fall on them; and they
will seize one another's hand, and the hand of one will
be lifted against the hand of another. Judah also will
fight at Jerusalem; and the wealth of all the surrounding
nations will be gathered, gold and silver and garments
in great abundance" (Zechariah 14:1-4, 12-14).

If you believe in the false separation between "the
rapture" and Second Coming, then you believe that the
Mount of Olives remains unchanged at "the rapture." But
if you believe that "the rapture," better understood as the
translation of the saints, and the Second Coming, are part
of the *same event* (cf. 2 Thessalonians 2:1), then you
indeed believe that the Mount of Olives is transformed.

Pre-tribulationists are incorrect in stating that Yeshua
will meet anyone at the Mount of Olives, as no Biblical
evidence is offered for this. The Scripture passage quoted
above from Zechariah, indicates that when the Messiah
returns the Mount of Olives will be split and that the
those who are occupying Jerusalem *will flee the city*, only
later to be defeated by Him. This is not a proof for pre-
tribulationism by any means.

**40. At the time of the rapture the Mount of Olives is
unchanged, while at the second coming it divides and a valley
is formed to the east of Jerusalem (Zech. 14:4-5).**

Consistent with what has already been stated in the
previous reason, if you believe in the separation between
"the rapture" and Second Coming and are pre-
tribulational, then you assume that the Mount of Olives
remains unchanged at "the rapture." But, if you believe
that the translation of the saints and Second Coming are
part of the same event, then you affirm that when these
Believers meet Yeshua in the clouds and return to Earth
with Him, that when He touches foot on the Mount of
Olives that it will indeed split—as the Scriptures plainly
state:

"In that day His feet will stand on the Mount of Olives, which is in front of Jerusalem on the east; and the Mount of Olives will be split in its middle from east to west by a very large valley, so that half of the mountain will move toward the north and the other half toward the south. You will flee by the valley of My mountains, for the valley of the mountains will reach to Azel; yes, you will flee just as you fled before the earthquake in the days of Uzziah king of Judah. Then the LORD, my God, will come, *and* all the holy ones with Him!" (Zechariah 14:4-5).

As also stated above, when Yeshua returns and when this valley is formed that those occupying Jerusalem will flee, only to be later met by Him at the Battle of Armageddon (cf. Revelation 16:16), detailed in the later verses of Zechariah 14.

41. At the rapture living saints are translated, while no saints are translated in connection with the second coming of Christ to the earth.

If this is true, and no living saints are translated at the Messiah's Second Coming or *parousia*, then why does the Apostle Paul speak of "the coming of our Lord Jesus Christ and our being gathered to him" (2 Thessalonians 2:1, NIV)? The *parousia*, the grand arrival of our Master, is when the "lawless one" will be "[slain] with the breath of His mouth and [brought] to an end by the appearance of His coming" (2 Thessalonians 2:8). If the *parousia* and our being gathered together to Yeshua are both parts of the same event, and the antimessiah/antichrist is defeated at this time, then why is a separation of these events made by pre-tribulationists? The Scriptures do not speak of such a separation. There will be a transformation of living saints and a resurrection of deceased saints; it will just take place at the end of the Tribulation. The escapism of pre-tribulationists is demonstrated by them ignoring the straightforward meaning of the text.

42. At the rapture the saints go to heaven, while at the second coming to the earth the saints remain in the earth without translation.

There is no Scripture text which states that at the Messiah's appearing the translated and transformed saints, who will received renewed bodies like His, are taken into Heaven. 1 Thessalonians 4:16-17 tells us, "the Lord Himself will descend from heaven with a shout, with the voice of *the* archangel and with the trumpet of God, and the dead in Messiah will rise first. Then we who are alive and remain will be caught up together with them in the clouds to meet the Lord in the air, and so we shall always be with the Lord." On the contrary, at the return of Yeshua He will return with a company of saints, those who have died in faith who will be reunited with their physical bodies: "the coming of our Lord Yeshua with all His saints" (1 Thessalonians 3:13). It is only at the return of the Messiah to the Earth that all saints, deceased and living, will finally be united together.

The Apostle Paul writes that the dead in Messiah will be first to be translated, and then the living saints will follow them. All will be caught up *en nephelais* (ἐν νεφέλαις) and *eis aera* (εἰς ἀέρα), "in clouds" and "in air." This has already been commented on in *When Will the Messiah Return?*:

> In 1 Thessalonians 4:17, Paul asserts that the righteous will "meet the Lord in the air." To some, it may seem that this meeting is only an "encountering." But what actually will occur is much more involved. The Greek term that is translated "meet" in this verse is *apantēsis* (ἀπάντησις). Vine notes that it "is used in the papyri of a newly arriving magistrate,"[66] in reference of course to its ancient classical usage. A notable place where *apantēsis* is used in the Apostolic Scriptures is Acts 28:15:

---

[66] W.E. Vine, *Expository Dictionary of Old and New Testament Words* (Nashville: Thomas Nelson, 1997), 730.

"And the brethren, when they heard about us, came from there as far as the Market of Appius and Three Inns to meet [apantēsis] us[67]; and when Paul saw them, he thanked God and took courage."

This verse speaks of the Believers in Rome going out to meet Paul as far as the Market of Appius and the Three Inns,[68] and then according to Acts 28:16, "we came into Rome" (RSV). This usage of apantēsis is an excellent indication that at His return, (1) the "meeting" involves Yeshua's coming to Earth to establish His throne, (2) that the saints will be gathered up into the clouds to meet Him, and (3) immediately following the company of redeemed will all go back to the Earth together. Just as the Roman Believers met Paul just outside of the city, and they all entered into Rome together—so will the righteous (those just resurrected and those transformed) meet the Lord and return to the Earth with Him.

Yeshua is indeed returning as a newly appointed magistrate to this planet, and He will establish the Torah as its constitution. He will rule in power and majesty as the Psalmist tells us: "You shall break them with a rod of iron, You shall shatter them like earthenware" (Psalm 2:9). The Prophet Isaiah further says, "it will come about that in the last days the mountain of the house of the LORD will be established as the chief of the mountains, and will be raised above the hills; and all the nations will stream to it. And many peoples will come and say, 'Come, let us go up to the mountain of the LORD, to the house of the God of Jacob; that He may teach us concerning His ways and that we may walk in His paths.' For the law will go forth from Zion and the word of the LORD from Jerusalem" (Isaiah 2:2-3; cf. Micah 4:2).

I sincerely hope that a select few of us, living at this time, may persevere long enough to be among those privileged ones who get to meet the Messiah in the clouds—*never having died*—as He comes to restore His Kingdom on Earth![69]

---

[67] Grk. *ēlthan eis apantēsin hēmin* (ἦλθαν εἰς ἀπάντησιν ἡμῖν); more lit. "came to a meeting with us" (Robert K. Brown and Philip W. Comfort, trans., *The New Greek-English Interlinear New Testament* [Carol Stream, IL: Tyndale House, 1990], 527).

[68] Some versions have Three Taverns.

[69] McKee, *WWTMR*, pp 23-24.

When Yeshua returns to gather the saints, they will not all go into Heaven, but rather meet Him in the clouds of the sky and then return to the Earth as He establishes His Kingdom, defeating His enemies. All the righteous saints in Heaven, though, will finally return to the Earth in the resurrection![70]

43. At the time of the rapture the world is unjudged and continues in sin, while at the second coming the world is judged and righteousness is established in the earth.

This reason is based on the false assertion that the gathering of the saints and Second Coming are separate events. The reasoning here is not based on Scripture but on assumption. Since we do not believe in the separation between "the rapture" and Second Coming, we cannot accept this as a proof for pre-tribulationism. As previously demonstrated in this publication, the gathering of the saints and Yeshua's *parousia* are both part of the same event, and as such when the Messiah returns to collect the living saints, He will likewise return to judge the world and establish His Millennial Kingdom.

---

[70] For a further discussion, with much more detailed analysis regarding the Tanach or Old Testament intertexuality present, consult the relevant sections of the author's commentary *1&2 Thessalonians for the Practical Messianic.* Also consult the author's forthcoming publication *The Resurrection and the Age to Come.*

Another excellent study to consider is N.T. Wright, *The Resurrection of the Son of God* (Minneapolis: Fortress Press, 2003).

44. The translation of the church is pictured as deliverance before the day of wrath, while the second coming is followed by the deliverance of those who have believed in Christ during the tribulation.

We have already commented on the correct connotation of "wrath" that Believers are spared from. The wrath that Believers are spared from is the *orgē* of God, the Greek word used in 1 Thessalonians 5:9 which tells us that "God has not destined us for wrath" (cf. Romans 5:9; 1 Thessalonians 1:10). Each time *orgē* is used in the Book of Revelation it is most often in a post-tribulational context. It is important that we review these passages:

- *Orgē* **occurs after the sixth seal, when the sky opens up and Yeshua returns to judge the world:** "The sky was split apart like a scroll when it is rolled up, and every mountain and island were moved out of their places. Then the kings of the earth and the great men and the commanders and the rich and the strong and every slave and free man hid themselves in the caves and among the rocks of the mountains; and they said to the mountains and to the rocks, 'Fall on us and hide us from the presence of Him who sits on the throne, and from the wrath [*orgē*] of the Lamb; for the great day of their wrath [*orgē*] has come, and who is able to stand?'" (Revelation 6:14-17).

- *Orgē* **occurs in reference to the seventh or last trumpet when the kingdoms of the world become those of the Lord:** "Then the seventh angel sounded; and there were loud voices in heaven, saying, 'The kingdom of the world has become *the kingdom* of our Lord and of His Messiah;

and He will reign forever and ever'....And the nations were enraged, and Your wrath [*orgē*] came, and the time *came* for the dead to be judged, and *the time* to reward Your bond-servants the prophets and the saints and those who fear Your name, the small and the great, and to destroy those who destroy the earth" (Revelation 11:15, 18).

- *Orgē* is poured out on the world as Yeshua defeats His enemies at Armageddon: "From His mouth comes a sharp sword, so that with it He may strike down the nations, and He will rule them with a rod of iron; and He treads the wine press of the fierce wrath [*orgē*][71] of God, the Almighty" (Revelation 19:15).

No one who has salvation in Messiah Yeshua will be subject to the *orgē* of God. According to pre-tribulationists, who believe that the entire Tribulation is the "wrath of God," the Tribulation saints who are saved during this period would actually experience the wrath of God. But Biblically this cannot possibly be the case if the saints are never to be subjected to God's wrath of eternal condemnation, and as we have demonstrated, the *orgē* of God in relation to the Messiah's return occurs in a post-tribulational context. Yeshua's Second Coming will be deliverance from the ***post-tribulational orgē*** that is to be delivered upon the world.

45. The rapture is described as imminent, while the second coming is preceded by definite signs.

We have already responded to this and stated that the Scriptures state that Messiah followers will not know the "day and hour" (Matthew 24:36, 50; Mark 13:32). This

---

[71] Actually appearing as *tou thumou tēs orgēs* (τοῦ θυμοῦ τῆς ὀργῆς), "the fury of the wrath" (NIV).

does not imply an "any moment," *imminent* return of the Messiah by any means; it simply means that they will not know the *exact* time of His return. As we have likewise already commented, 2 Thessalonians 2:1-4 states that before Yeshua can return the apostasy and the revealing of the antimessiah/antichrist must occur.

It is right to say that the Second Coming is preceded by definite signs. However, the problem for pre-tribulationists is that there is no Scriptural support for separating the "rapture" from the Second Coming; both are part of the *same event.*

46. The translation of living believers is truth revealed only in the New Testament, while the second coming with its attendant events is a prominent doctrine of both Testaments.

The primary prophetic passage from the Tanach (Old Testament), used in reference to the resurrection, is Daniel 12:2, "Many of those who sleep in the dust of the ground will awake, these to everlasting life, but the others to disgrace *and* everlasting contempt." This verse speaks of a resurrection of both the righteous, to everlasting communion with the Lord in renewed bodies, and for the unrighteous, to everlasting separation from the Lord in renewed bodies.

It is correct to assert that only in the Apostolic Scriptures is the translation of *living* Believers revealed. As quoted numerous times in this publication already, Paul says in 1 Corinthians 15:51, "Behold, I tell you a mystery; we will not all sleep, but we will all be changed." But simply because this is not revealed to us in the Tanach (Old Testament) in such stated terms does not automatically mean that there is a pre-tribulation rapture. There are other things revealed to God's people in the Apostolic Scriptures which are not revealed in the Tanach Scriptures. Hebrews 1:1 indicates, "In many and various ways God spoke of old to our fathers by the prophets" (RSV). There is such a thing as *progressive revelation*. God has continually revealed new things to His people in the course of history, such as the translation of *living Believers* at the time of Yeshua's return as opposed to just those who are deceased.

Of course, 1 Corinthians 15:52 asserts that this translation of the saints occurs at the "last trumpet," and we know the seventh trumpet of Revelation 11:15 is when the kingdoms of the world become those of Yeshua—indicating that this takes place at His Second Coming and arrival to the Earth to establish His Millennial reign. This can be easily reconciled with Daniel's words because 1 Thessalonians 4:16 tells us that "the dead in Messiah will rise first." We are then told after this, "Then we who are alive and remain will be caught up together with them in the clouds to meet the Lord in the air, and so we shall always be with the Lord" (1 Thessalonians 4:17).

It is correct to assume that the Tanach speaks of many things to occur following the Second Coming of the Messiah, but pre-tribulationists are being highly selective in claiming that since the translation of living Believers is not expressly stated in the Tanach that there is a pre-tribulation rapture. Again, there are things in the New Testament not fully revealed in the Old Testament, emphasizing that the Lord has continually shown *new* things to His people over time, **but** progressive revelation via the unfolding of salvation history is a far cry from dispensationalism, where God has a Plan A for Israel and a Plan B for "the Church."[72]

47. The rapture concerns only the saved, while the second coming deals with both saved and unsaved.

This support for pre-tribulationism is based on the false separation assumed to exist between "the rapture" and Second Coming. Since as post-tribulationists we

---

[72] Consult the author's comments on Hebrews 1:1-2 in his commentary *Hebrews for the Practical Messianic*.

believe that the translation of the saints and Yeshua's Second Coming are both part of the same event (cf. 2 Thessalonians 2:1), we do not accept it as being legitimate.

Another way to assert our position in view of the claim given above, is that the gathering into the clouds to meet Yeshua—the resurrection of deceased saints' bodies and translation of living Believers—is only for the saved, and the subsequent Second Coming involves Believers returning with the Lord and a company of unsaved who are defeated at the Battle of Armageddon.

48. At the rapture Satan is not bound, while at the second coming Satan is bound and cast into the abyss.

This is a false assertion because pre-tribulationists, once again, falsely believe that "the rapture" and Second Coming are separate events. Since we do not believe these presuppositions to be Biblical, we do not accept this as a viable support of pre-tribulationism. The antimessiah/antichrist and false prophet are defeated and thrown into the Lake of Fire, and Satan is clearly bound and thrown into the bottomless pit for a thousand years at Yeshua's Second Coming, which occur in conjunction with the translation and gathering of the saints:

> "And the beast was seized, and with him the false prophet who performed the signs in his presence, by which he deceived those who had received the mark of the beast and those who worshiped his image; these two were thrown alive into the lake of fire which burns with brimstone" (Revelation 19:20).

> "And he laid hold of the dragon, the serpent of old, who is the devil and Satan, and bound him for a thousand years; and he threw him into the abyss, and shut *it* and sealed *it* over him, so that he would not deceive the nations any longer, until the thousand years were completed; after these things he must be released for a short time" (Revelation 20:2-3).

49. No unfufilled prophecy stands between the church and the rapture, while many signs must be fulfilled before the second coming.

There are some significant prophecies that must occur between now and the return of Yeshua for the *ekklēsia*/assembly and His Second Coming. Read the Olivet Discourse first from Matthew 24, and then the parallel accounts in Mark 13 and Luke 21. All of these passages communicate how the Messiah will gather His elect "after the tribulation." These passages only scratch the surface in regard to the end-time prophecies which occur before Yeshua's *parousia*. But, the manifold Scripture texts that we would say have prophecies that must occur before the *parousia* are disregarded by pre-tribulationists because of their errant separation of Israel and the so-called "Church."

50. No passage dealing with the resurrection of saints at the second coming in either Testament ever mentions translation of living saints at the same time.

This last support provided is very closely connected to the false ecclesiology of pre-tribulationists who believe that "the Church" is a group of elect totally separate and independent from Israel. And, it forgets the reality that there is progressive revelation throughout the Scriptures (Hebrews 1:1-2). It is taught by many pre-tribulationists that the resurrection of the dead involved with the pre-tribulation rapture only involves deceased members of "the Church," by their definition, and not members of Israel. They apply verses from the Apostolic Writings on the gathering of the saints and resurrection to "the Church," but consider the Tanach (Old Testament) references on the resurrection to apply only to Israel, again by their definition, and not to them. Thus Daniel 12:2 only speaks of the resurrection of "Israelite saints," so to speak, and not to "Church saints." This, by pre-tribulationists' logic, can only be true because Daniel 12:2 is very clearly in a post-tribulational context: "Many of those who sleep in the dust of the ground will awake, these to everlasting life, but the others to disgrace *and* everlasting contempt."

We have already answered this claim in *When Will the Messiah Return?*:

> Of this verse, John F. Walvoord actually observes,
>
> "It has been characterized of some branches of premillenarians to include the resurrection of Israel [represented in this passage] with the resurrection of the church at the time of the rapture. Those who have followed this interpretation have been somewhat embarrassed by the fact that Daniel 12:1,2 seems to place the resurrection of Israel after the tribulation instead of before it. This would indicate that...the rapture is posttribulational in that the resurrection follows the tribulation."[73]
>
> Those who are dispensational like Walvoord, and who believe that God has two groups of elect, have difficulty with the assertion of Daniel 12:2. Those who are not dispensational, and who believe that all of the righteous are a part of Israel—meaning that non-Jewish Believers too are a part of Israel's Commonwealth (Ephesians 2:11-13), the Israel of God (Galatians 6:16), and are grafted-in by their Messiah faith (Romans 11:17)—would affirm that all of the righteous get resurrected at the same time. And as such, the resurrection of the righteous mentioned in Daniel 12:2 **must be the resurrection of all of the elect who are in the Lord.**
>
> Walvoord himself believes that the resurrections of the righteous and the condemned occur at different times, as Revelation 20:5 says: "The rest of the dead did not come to life until the thousand years were completed." He comments, "A paraphrase would render [Daniel 12:2] this way: 'Many of them that sleep in the dust of the earth shall awake, these to everlasting life, and those to shame and everlasting contempt.' The passage...becomes a statement that subsequent to the tribulation all the dead will be raised, but in two

---

[73] John F. Walvoord, *Israel In Prophecy* (Grand Rapids: Zondervan, 1962), 116.

groups, one group to everlasting life and the other group to everlasting contempt. The fact that these are separated in time is clearly spelled out in Revelation 20, and the fact that this detail is not given here should not be considered a major problem."[74] The resurrection of the condemned would occur after the thousand year Millennial reign of the Messiah on Earth.

Given the importance of Daniel 12:2 for the doctrine of resurrection, and how it acknowledges two resurrections to occur—one for the righteous, and one for the condemned—then if the resurrection for the righteous in this verse is only for ethnic Israel or the Jewish people, where do members of some separate "Church" entity get resurrected? Pre-tribulationists will widely and correctly conclude that the second resurrection, the resurrection of the condemned in Daniel 12:2, is the same as in Revelation 20:5. Should we not also conclude, then, that the resurrection of the righteous in Daniel 12:2 is the same one spoken of in the Apostolic Scriptures in the critical "rapture passages"?

Why would God confuse His own, in having two resurrections for the righteous—but then only one for the condemned? *This is what pre-tribulationists widely conclude.* Could it simply be that pre-tribulationists are following a flawed hermeneutic which advocates their desire to want to "get out" at the earliest possible moment, and they will bend Scripture to prove so?

There will only be two bodily resurrections: one for the righteous, and the other for the condemned. Yeshua said in John 5:28-29, "Do not marvel at this; for an hour is coming, in which all who are in the tombs will hear His voice, and will come forth; those who did the good *deeds* to a resurrection of life, those who committed the evil *deeds* to a resurrection of judgment." This is fully consistent with the prophecy of Daniel 12:2, as some will be resurrected to an existence of grand communion with their Creator in the coming New Creation—and others will be resurrected to a final sentencing for crimes committed against their Creator. The resurrection of the righteous is clearly a post-tribulational event, and it is for all the righteous.[75]

---

[74] Ibid., 117.
[75] McKee, *WWTMR*, pp 26-28.

This concludes our responses to Walvoord's fifty reasons in support of pre-tribulationism. We have demonstrated from Scripture, and from a Messianic ecclesiology of all Believers being a part of the community or Kingdom realm of Israel, that pre-tribulationism is flawed. We have shown where pre-tribulationists take various verses out of context to support what is largely an escapist desire to leave at the first sign of trouble. We have exposed some pre-tribulationists as manipulating the Bible for their own ends.

Most importantly, we hope that the refutations to Walvoord have demonstrated the need for us to prepare for the coming times ahead, and how today's Messianic Believers need to have a strong foundation in the Word of God—most especially the Torah—as the Torah shows us the pattern of what is to come in the Last Days. As the Apostle Paul tells us, "these things happened to them as a warning, but they were written down for our instruction, upon whom the end of the ages has come" (1 Corinthians 10:11, RSV).

▪4▪

WHY ARE WE
POST-TRIB?

We have just examined some of the major flaws in the pre-tribulation rapture teaching. We have responded to many of the arguments given by its major proponents, and we sincerely hope you see where they are misguided. We affirm the opposite view, which is that Believers will remain on Planet Earth during the Tribulation period. We do not believe that it is the pattern of Scripture, especially the Torah, for God to give His people an "easy escape," but rather for them to be protected by Him and rely on Him during times of distress. Whether many pre-tribulationists wish to admit it or not, *their fear of the Last Days and of the times to come* is what largely motivates them—not necessarily their faith in the Lord. It would be my personal hope, though, that I am wrong in this assertion.

It is not without reservation that we explain why we hold to a post-tribulational view of the gathering of the saints. This is by far the most controversial position one could take, **as we are saying that Believers may be forced to give up their lives one day for the cause of the Messiah and face the antimessiah/antichrist.** Some pre-tribulationists say that a post-tribulational view of the end-times does not encourage spiritual growth and creates "lukewarm Believers." This is absolutely ludicrous considering the fact that many of us, including myself, may one day have to be martyred for the cause of

Yeshua. Being a "lukewarm" Believer is hardly something that I would consider myself to be. As a Messianic Believer, I know that it is important to hold to the testimony of Yeshua and keep the commandments of God (Revelation 12:17; 14:12), something that the Tribulation saints do, and a significant number of pre-tribulationists today do not necessarily do. Are post-tribulationism's pre-trib accusers willing to face the antimessiah and be martyred? Are they willing to live a set-apart lifestyle and heed the messages of God's Torah? Even though our ministry is post-trib, we do not instinctively want to experience the Tribulation. *We hope that we are wrong!* However, Scripture shows us that we are (probably) not wrong, and we pray that we may have the strength to endure the times ahead—whatever happens, and even if all we may face is general tribulation.

As emphasized throughout this publication, TNN Online and Outreach Israel Ministries affirm a belief in a post-tribulation gathering of the saints for two specific reasons:

1. We **do not believe** that "the Church" and Israel are separate entities. We believe that God has only one group of chosen ones, the Commonwealth of Israel (Ephesians 2:11-12) or the Israel of God (Galatians 6:16), composing Jewish and non-Jewish Believers, with non-Jewish Believers grafted-in to Israel's olive tree by faith (Romans 11:16-17). As the Tribulation period is in actuality the Seventieth Week of Israel, and as Believers are a part of Israel's polity, we will all remain on Planet Earth during its duration.[1]

---

[1] For a further analysis of ecclesiology, consult the author's publication, *Are Non-Jewish Believers Really a Part of Israel?* (forthcoming 2013).

2. Yeshua the Messiah plainly tells us that He
    returns "**after the tribulation** of those days"
    (Matthew 24:29-31; cf. Mark 13:24-27; Luke
    21:27-28).

Dispensationalists who see "the Church" and Israel as
separate entities obviously do not consider that non-
Jewish Believers in Israel's Messiah will be participants,
directly (or even indirectly), involved in Israel's
prophecies, and therefore they see themselves removed
from the Seventieth Week of Israel. However, if Believers
are a part of the qahal/ekklēsia of Israel, then the
Tribulation is indeed for all of us. The Messiah Himself
attests,

"But immediately after the tribulation of those days
THE SUN WILL BE DARKENED, AND THE MOON WILL NOT GIVE
ITS LIGHT, AND THE STARS WILL FALL from the sky, and the
powers of the heavens will be shaken. And then the sign
of the Son of Man will appear in the sky, and then all the
tribes of the earth will mourn, and they will see the SON
OF MAN COMING ON THE CLOUDS OF THE SKY with power
and great glory. And He will send forth His angels with A
GREAT TRUMPET and THEY WILL GATHER TOGETHER His elect
from the four winds, from one end of the sky to the
other" (Matthew 24:29-31).

When one reads the entire chapter of Matthew 24 in
context, one cannot come to the conclusion that the pre-
tribulation rapture is a teaching of our Lord. If the event
in Matthew 24:29-31 (cf. Mark 13:24-27; Luke 21:27-28)
is not "the rapture" as it is commonly called, as the saints
are gathered into the sky, then what is it? We choose to
stand on Yeshua the Messiah's words which speak of a
post-tribulational gathering of all the saints, and interpret
all other words **through His words!** The Apostle Paul
himself said that correct teaching is properly viewed
through the Messiah's teachings (1 Timothy 6:3).

It can easily be argued that many Christians have
been deceived by the pre-tribulation rapture teaching,
especially in view of their attitude and approach to the
Last Days. What will they do if their doctrine is wrong

and they find themselves in the Tribulation period and its hardships? Will they stand for the Messiah—possibly having to lose their lives? Or will they join the antimessiah/antichrist? *It is not our job to judge the heart intent of the pre-tribulationist.* Rather, it is the pre-tribulationist's job to study and evaluate whether or not this view is truly upheld by the Word of God, and take their questions and concerns before Him.

Our Heavenly Father is all-powerful and all-knowing. We do not claim to know the exact time of Yeshua's return—nor do we believe it is justified to try to calculate the time of His return—but we do see major problems with the widely accepted pre-tribulation rapture teaching. If you are a pre-tribulationist, I urge you to reconsider your position.

These are our conclusions, as a ministry, based on Scripture, prayer, and cautious reasoning. If indeed our position is proven to be wrong and there is a pre-tribulation rapture, **then we will gladly accept it.** As many have observed, "I hope for the best, but I prepare for the worst." But if we are right, and you are a pre-tribulationist, you are likely to have to answer for it.

Consider what you have read and examine it. Are our conclusions correct? Challenge us where you feel we have gone wrong and we will certainly be open to hearing you. Give us additional reasons that we can add to future editions of this analysis. Give us ideological support for pre-tribulationism that is not escapist, and show us where Yeshua telling us He gathers the saints after the Tribulation is out of place.

About the Author

John Kimball Mckee is the founder and principal writer for TNN Online, an Internet website that specializes in a wide variety of Biblical topics. He has grown up in a family that has been in constant pursuit of God's truth, and has been exposed to things of the Lord since infancy. Since 1995 he has come to the realization of the post-tribulational return of the Messiah for His own and the importance of our Hebraic Roots. He is a graduate of the University of Oklahoma (Class of 2003) with a B.A. in political science, and holds an M.A. in Biblical Studies from Asbury Theological Seminary (Class of 2009). He is a 2009 recipient of the Zondervan Biblical Languages Award for Greek. John holds memberships in the Evangelical Theological Society and the Evangelical Philosophical Society.

John is an apologist for the Creator God and in helping people understand their faith heritage in Ancient Israel and Second Temple Judaism. Much of his ministry in the past has been campus based to the multitudes in evangelical Christianity who are associated with a wide variety of Protestant denominations and persuasions. John has introduced college students to things that are Messianic such as the original Hebrew name of our Savior, Yeshua HaMashiach (Jesus the Messiah), a name that he has known since 1983.

John's testimony before his Christian friends at college challenged much of their previous thinking about the whole of the Holy Scriptures and the need to follow the commandments of the Most High. His college peers asked him many questions: Why do you not believe in the pre-trib rapture? What do you think of the *Left Behind* books? Why do you observe the seventh-day Sabbath? Why do you eat kosher? Why do you wear a beard? Why do you celebrate the feasts of Israel? Why will you use a *tallit* and wrap *tefillin*/phylacteries during private prayer? Why do you consult original Hebrew and Greek language texts of the Bible? Why don't you come to church with us on Sunday? This led John into Messianic apologetics and the defense of our faith. John strives to be one who is committed to a life of holiness and methodical Bible study, as a person who has a testimony of being born again and who sincerely desires to obey the Lord.

As the editor of TNN Online, John's ministry has capitalized on the Internet's ability to reach people all over this planet. The Theology News Network speaks with challenging, provocative, and apologetic articles to a wide Messianic audience, and those Christians who are interested in Messianic beliefs. In the past decade, TNN Online has emerged as a moderate and Centrist voice in a Messianic movement that is trying to determine its purpose, relevance, and mission to modern society. John feels a strong calling to assist in the development and maturation of our emerging Messianic theology. John has had the profound opportunity since 1997 to engage many in dialogue, so that they will consider the questions he postulates, as his only agenda is to be as Scripturally sound as possible. John believes in demonstrating a great deal of honor and respect to both his evangelical Christian, Wesleyan and Reformed heritage, as well as to the Jewish Synagogue, and together allowing the strengths of both Judaism and Christianity to be employed for the Lord's plan for the Messianic movement in the long term future.

J.K. McKee is author of numerous books, dealing with a wide range of topics that are important for today's Messianic Believers. He has also written many articles on theological issues, and is presently focusing his attention on Messianic commentaries of various books of the Bible.

J.K. McKee is the son of the late K. Kimball McKee (1951-1992) and Margaret Jeffries McKee Huey (1953-), and stepson of William Mark Huey (1951-), who married his mother in 1994, and is the executive director of Outreach Israel Ministries.

John has a very strong appreciation for those who have preceded him. His father, Kimball McKee, was a licensed lay minister in the Kentucky Conference of the United Methodist Church, and was a very strong evangelical Christian, most appreciable of the Hebraic and Jewish Roots of the faith. Among his many ministry pursuits, Kim brought the Passover *sedar* to Christ United Methodist Church in Florence, KY, was a Sunday school teacher, and was extremely active in the Walk to Emmaus, leading the first men's walk in Madras, India in 1991. John is the grandson of the late William W. Jeffries (1914-1989), who served as a professor at the United States Naval Academy in Annapolis, MD from 1942-1989, notably as the museum director and founder of what is now the William W. Jeffries Memorial Archives in the Nimitz Library. John is the great-grandson of Bishop Marvin A. Franklin (1894-1972), who served as a minister and bishop of the Methodist Church, throughout his ministry serving churches in Georgia, Florida, Alabama, and Mississippi. Bishop Franklin was President of the Council of Bishops from 1959-1960. John is also the third cousin of the late Charles L. Allen (1913-2005), formerly the senior pastor of Grace Methodist Church of Atlanta, GA and First Methodist Church of Houston, TX, and author of numerous books, notably including *God's Psychiatry*. Among all of his forbearers, though, he considers his personality to be most derived from his late paternal grandfather, George Kenneth McKee (1903-1978), and his maternal grandmother, Mary Ruth Franklin Jeffries (1919-).

J.K. McKee is a native of the Northern Kentucky/Greater Cincinnati, OH area. He has also lived in Dallas, TX, Norman, OK, Kissimmee-St. Cloud, FL, and Roatán, Honduras, Central America.

APPENDIX

HOW WILL THE WORLD COME TOGETHER?

One day soon the Lord Jesus Christ will come. He will gather all those millions who know Him into the clouds in the rapture. Because so many will disappear, cars will be without drivers, planes will be without pilots, and infrastructure will come to a standstill. So many people will be missing that the world will be forced to unite.

How many of us have been taught something like this? How many of us have been told that the only thing that will bring Planet Earth together and inaugurate a massive world government will be the rapture?

In recent days, especially during the late 1990s, speculation about world government among Believers has been at an all time high. Following World War II and with the Cold War, it seemed unlikely that world government could occur. The Cold War polarized the world between the power centers of Washington and Moscow. The United Nations was nothing less than a debating chamber for the two superpowers and their proxy states. Western European integration might have been occurring at the same time, but this was largely due to post-World War II devastation and an effort to revitalize Europe's economies through integration. Suffice it to say, world government was the last thing on anyone's minds.

Following the collapse of the Soviet Union, nation-states of the world are now in a more viable position to seek greater unity. The prime element behind globalization and the global community is a drive to see greater exchange of goods and an expanse of trade. With global communications and the Internet, people all over the world are able to share information and ideas. With the initiation of the euro, there is now a single currency for the world's largest market, the European Union. We are definitely moving toward greater world integration. One day, as the Scriptures tell us, there will be world government and a single world leader:

"Thus he said: 'The fourth beast will be a fourth kingdom on the earth, which will be different from all the *other* kingdoms and will devour the whole earth and tread it down and crush it. As for the ten horns, out of this kingdom ten kings will arise; and another will arise after them, and he will be different from the previous ones and will subdue three kings. He will speak out against the Most High and wear down the saints of the Highest One, and he will intend to make alterations in times and in law; and they will be given into his hand for a time, times, and half a time'" (Daniel 7:23-25).

The question that is being asked by many prophecy teachers right now is not necessarily "Will the world come together?" This much should be obvious if you read the Bible and believe in the literal fulfillment of prophecy. The question being asked is "How will the world come together?" Suffice it to say, everyone has his own theory or opinion about how the world will come together.

A predominant view in evangelical Christianity right now is that the rapture will happen, millions of people will suddenly disappear, and societal anarchy will ensue—thus causing the world to unite, via the arrival of the antimessiah/antichrist.

Is there a problem with this scenario? Other than the fact that Yeshua the Messiah plainly tells us that He returns "after the tribulation" (Matthew 24:29-31) and Paul says He returns at "the last trumpet" (1 Corinthians 15:51-52)—yes, there is a serious problem. Other than the fact that the pre-tribulation rapture is *not supported* by

Scripture, how do we know that in the event a pre-trib rapture were to occur that there would be enough people missing for it to even matter? This is not a trick question. How many people in Christianity are even "saved" so that they would be taken up into the clouds to meet Yeshua? If you were thinking billions, then I believe you are mistaken. Many American Christians today are *unwilling to experience the Tribulation or hard times*, which speaks volumes as to their salvation experience and if they truly have faith in God.

Many popular pre-tribulationists have done a good job at making people think that the pre-trib rapture is what is needed to cause societal anarchy and thus the rise of the antimessiah. But must it be the rapture that causes problems which lead to world unity? I do not believe so. I believe that there can be something much worse happen than the rapture that leads to chaos:

"For this reason in one day her plagues will come, pestilence and mourning and famine, and she will be burned up with fire; for the Lord God who judges her is strong. And the kings of the earth, who committed *acts of immorality* and lived sensuously with her, will weep and lament over her when they see the smoke of her burning, standing at a distance because of the fear of her torment, saying, 'Woe, woe, the great city, Babylon, the strong city! For in one hour your judgment has come'" (Revelation 18:8-10).

There are many prophecy teachers who believe that the end-time Babylonian phenomenon is more than just a world-wide system. There are those who believe that Revelation 18 speaks of a literal city, in fact, some believe that it speaks of New York City.[1] The implication among some prophecy teachers is that the city which is destroyed in one hour is New York—a city that is a center of world trade, industry, and diplomacy.

If September 11, 2001 has proven anything, it has proven that the world has new threats—like global

---

[1] Consult the author's article "The Babylons of Revelation 17 & 18."

terrorism. Terrorists want to do more than fly airplanes into buildings, because the more people they kill, the more people they scare, and the more they scare, the more they get an audience and a platform for their beliefs. Terrorists, be they Islamic terrorists or otherwise, want weapons of mass destruction. Consider an even worse scenario than the rapture taking millions of people to Heaven prior to the Tribulation period:

> *Leaders from all the United Nations member states were assembled in New York. They sat down at the conference, ready to discuss the issues at hand. Every one of them was prepared. And then it happened. We did not think it would happen, but it did. Terrorists exploded a nuclear bomb in the city of New York killing millions—including the world leaders, presidents, prime ministers, chancellors, executives, at the United Nations. The world is in a total state of shock and disarray as the leaders of the United States, Britain, France, Germany, Japan, Russia, India, China, and other countries were all slaughtered in a blink instant. The world will move on, but can there be a tragedy that tops this? Who was responsible? Whomever they are we will be a united world around _____ and we will make them pay.*

Considering our times, this is a plausible possibility on how the world could come together. Murder world leaders assembling together at a big gathering, and then open the door for a global tyrant to arise. More anarchy will be caused if world leaders are slaughtered all at once in a nuclear blast then if people just disappear via the pre-trib rapture.

We do not know exactly how the world will come together, giving rise to the antimessiah/antichrist. All we can do is speculate at the moment. But this brief commentary should demonstrate that a pre-tribulation rapture is not required to be the catalyst to enable the arrival and ascension of the man of lawlessness into power.

BIBLIOGRAPHY

Articles
Köster, H. *"tópos,"* in *TDNT.*
Sessemann, H. "test, attempt," in *TDNT.*

Bible Versions and Study Bibles
American Standard Version (New York: Thomas Nelson & Sons, 1901).
Barker, Kenneth L., ed., et. al. *NIV Study Bible* (Grand Rapids: Zondervan, 2002).
Berlin, Adele, and Marc Zvi Brettler, eds. *The Jewish Study Bible*, NJPS (Oxford: Oxford University Press, 2004).
Esposito, Paul W. *The Apostles' Bible, An English Septuagint Version* (http://www.apostlesbible.com/).
Green, Jay P., trans. *The Interlinear Bible* (Lafayette, IN: Sovereign Grace Publishers, 1986).
Harrelson, Walter J., ed., et. al. *New Interpreter's Study Bible*, NRSV (Nashville: Abingdon, 2003).
Holman Christian Standard Bible (Nashville: Broadman & Holman, 2004).
Holy Bible, Contemporary English Version (New York: American Bible Society, 1995).
Holy Bible, King James Version (edited 1789).
Holy Bible, New International Version (Grand Rapids: Zondervan, 1978).
LaHaye, Tim, ed. *Tim LaHaye Prophecy Study Bible*, KJV (Chattanooga: AMG Publishers, 2000).
New American Standard Bible (La Habra, CA: Foundation Press Publications, 1971).
Newman, Barclay M., ed. *Holy Bible: Contemporary English Version* (New York: American Bible Society, 1995).
New American Standard, Updated Edition (Anaheim, CA: Foundation Publications, 1995).
New English Bible (Oxford and Cambridge: Oxford and Cambridge University Presses, 1970).
New King James Version (Nashville: Thomas Nelson, 1982).
New Revised Standard Version (National Council of Churches of Christ, 1989).
Packer, J.I., ed. *The Holy Bible, English Standard Version* (Wheaton, IL: Crossway Bibles, 2001).
Ryrie, Charles C., ed. *The Ryrie Study Bible*, New American Standard (Chicago: Moody Press, 1978).
Scherman, Nosson, and Meir Zlotowitz, eds. *ArtScroll Tanach* (Brooklyn: Mesorah Publications, 1996).
Siewert, Frances E., ed. *The Amplified Bible* (Grand Rapids: Zondervan, 1965).

Stern, David H., trans. *Jewish New Testament* (Clarksville, MD: Jewish New Testament Publications, 1995).
_____, trans. *Complete Jewish Bible* (Clarksville, MD: Jewish New Testament Publications, 1998).
Tanakh: The Holy Scriptures (Philadelphia: Jewish Publication Society, 1999).
The Holy Bible, Revised Standard Version (Nashville: Cokesbury, 1952).
Young, Robert, trans. *Young's Literal Translation.*
Zodhiates, Spiros, ed. *Hebrew-Greek Key Study Bible*, NASB (Chattanooga: AMG Publishers, 1994).

Books and Booklets
Archer, Jr., Gleason L., and Paul D. Feinberg, Douglas J. Moo, Richard R. Reiter. *Three Views on the Rapture* (Grand Rapids: Zondervan, 1996).
Arnold, William. *The Post-Tribulation Rapture* (Stockton, CA: Author, 1999).
Boyd, Gregory A., and Paul R. Eddy. *Across the Spectrum: Understanding Issues in Evangelical Theology* (Grand Rapids: Baker Academic, 2002).
Erickson, Millard J. *Contemporary Options In Eschatology* (Grand Rapids: Baker Books, 1977).
Fructenbaum, Arnold G. *Israelology: The Missing Link in Systematic Theology*, revised edition (Tustin, CA: Ariel Ministries, 1996).
Gundry, Robert H. *The Church and the Tribulation* (Grand Rapids: Zondervan, 1973).
_____. *First the Antichrist* (Grand Rapids: Baker Books, 1997).
Hagee, John. *From Daniel to Doomsday* (Nashville: Thomas Nelson, 1999).
Hanegraaf, Hank. *The Bible Answer Book 2* (Nashville: Thomas Nelson, 2006).
Horton, Beka. *Book of Revelation, Church History, and Things to Come* (Pensacola: Pensacola Christian College, 1993).
Hunt, Dave. *How Close Are We?* (Eugene, OR: Harvest House Publishers, 1993).
Huey, William Mark, and J.K. McKee. *Hebraic Roots: An Introductory Study* (Kissimmee, FL: TNN Press, 2003).
Juster, Dan, and Keith Intrater. *Israel, the Church and the Last Days* (Shippensburg, PA: Destiny Image, 1990).
Juster, Daniel C. *Growing to Maturity* (Denver: The Union of Messianic Jewish Congregations Press, 1987).
_____. *Jewish Roots* (Shippensburg, PA: Destiny Image, 1995).
Ladd, George Eldon. *The Blessed Hope* (Grand Rapids: Eerdmans, 1956).
_____. *A Commentary on the Revelation of John* (Grand Rapids: Eerdmans, 1972).
LaHaye, Tim. *Rapture Under Attack: Will You Escape the Tribulation?* (Sisters, OR: Multnomah Publishers, 1998).
MacPherson, Dave. *The Rapture Plot* (Simpsonville, SC: Millennium III Publishers, 1994).

_____. The Three R's (Simpsonville, SC; P.O S.T. Inc.,
     1998).
McKee, J.K. Torah In the Balance, Volume I (Kissimmee, FL: TNN Press,
     2003).
_____. The New Testament Validates Torah (Kissimmee, FL: TNN
     Press, 2004).
_____. A Survey of the Apostolic Scriptures for the Practical
     Messianic (Kissimmee, FL: TNN Press, 2006).
_____. A Survey of the Tanach for the Practical Messianic
     (Kissimmee, FL: TNN Press, 2008).
_____. When Will the Messiah Return? (Kissimmee, FL: TNN Press,
     2009/2012).
Montgomery, Don. Rapture: Post-Tribulation and Pre-Wrath (Enumclaw,
     WA: WinePress Publishing, 1999).
Moseley, Ron. Yeshua: A Guide to the Real Jesus and the Original
     Church (Baltimore: Lederer Books, 1996).
Rasmussen, Roland. The Post-Trib, Pre-Wrath Rapture (Canoga Park, CA:
     The Post-Trib Research Center, 1996).
Rosenthal, Marvin. The Pre-Wrath Rapture of the Church (Nashville:
     Thomas Nelson, 1990).
Sadler, Paul. The Triumph of His Grace: Preparing Ourselves for the
     Rapture (Germantown, WI: Berean Bible Society, 1995).
Snell, Jay. No Thief Gives Warning Signs: The Death of the Mid and Post
     Tribulation Rapture Theories (Pearland, TX: Jay Snell Evangelistic
     Association, 1995).
Stam, C.R. Things That Differ (Germantown, WI: Berean Bible Society,
     1985).
Stern, David H. Messianic Jewish Manifesto (Clarksville, MD: Jewish
     New Testament Publications, 1992).
Strandberg, Todd, and Terry James. Are You Rapture Ready? (New York:
     Dutton, 2003).
Van Impe, Jack. The Great Escape (Nashville: Thomas Nelson, 1998).
Van Kampen, Robert. The Rapture Question Answered (Grand Rapids:
     Fleming H. Revell, 1997).
Walvoord, John F. The Rapture Question (Grand Rapids: Zondervan,
     1956).
_____. Israel In Prophecy (Grand Rapids: Zondervan, 1962).
_____. The Church In Prophecy (Grand Rapids: Zondervan,
     1964).
_____. The Nations In Prophecy (Grand Rapids: Zondervan,
     1967).
_____. Every Prophecy of the Bible (Colorado Springs:
     Chariot Victor Publishing, 1999).
Wilson, Marvin R. Our Father Abraham (Grand Rapids: Eerdmans,
     1989).
Wright, N.T. Surprised by Hope: Rethinking Heaven, the Resurrection,
     and the Mission of the Church (New York: HarperCollins, 2008).

Christian Reference Sources and Cited Commentaries
Alexander, T. Desmond, and David W. Baker, eds. *Dictionary of the Old Testament Pentateuch* (Downers Grove, IL: InterVarsity, 2003).
Arnold, Bill T., and H.G.M. Williamson, eds. *Dictionary of the Old Testament Historical Books* (Downers Grove, IL: InterVarsity, 2005).
Bercot, David W., ed. *A Dictionary of Early Christian Beliefs* (Peabody, MA: Hendrickson Publishers, 1998).
Bromiley, Geoffrey, ed. *International Standard Bible Encyclopedia*, 4 vols. (Grand Rapids: Eerdmans, 1988).
Buttrick, George, ed. et. al. *The Interpreter's Dictionary of the Bible*, 4 vols. (Nashville: Abingdon, 1962).
Cairns, Alan. *Dictionary of Theological Terms* (Greenville, SC: Ambassador Emerald International, 2002).
Crim, Keith, ed. *Interpreter's Dictionary of the Bible: Supplementary Volume* (Nashville: Abingdon, 1976).
Evans, Craig A., and Stanley E. Porter, eds. *Dictionary of New Testament Background* (Downers Grove, IL: InterVarsity, 2000).
Freedman, David Noel, ed. *Anchor Bible Dictionary*, 6 vols. (New York: Doubleday, 1992).
Gaebelein, Frank E., ed. et. al. *Expositor's Bible Commentary*, 12 vols. (Grand Rapids: Zondervan, 1976-1992).
Geisler, Norman L., ed. *Baker Encyclopedia of Christian Apologetics* (Grand Rapids: Baker, 1999).
Green, Joel B., Scot McKnight, and I. Howard Marshall, eds. *Dictionary of Jesus and the Gospels* (Downers Grove, IL: InterVarsity, 1992).
Grenz, Stanley J., David Guretzki, and Cherith Fee Nordling. *Pocket Dictionary of Theological Terms* (Downers Grove, IL: InterVarsity, 1999).
Guthrie, D. and J.A. Motyer, eds. *The New Bible Commentary Revised* (Grand Rapids: Eerdmans, 1970).
Harrison, Everett F., ed. *Baker's Dictionary of Theology* (Grand Rapids: Baker Book House, 1960).
Hawthorne, Gerald F., Ralph P. Martin, and Daniel G. Reid, eds. *Dictionary of Paul and His Letters* (Downers Grove, IL: InterVarsity, 1993).
Keener, Craig S. *The IVP Bible Background Commentary: New Testament* (Downers Grove, IL: InterVarsity, 1993).
_____. *NIV Application Commentary: Revelation* (Grand Rapids: Zondervan, 2000).
Keil, C., and F. Delitzsch, eds. *Commentary on the Old Testament*, 10 vols.
Laymon, Charles M., ed. *The Interpreter's One-Volume Commentary on the Bible* (Nashville: Abingdon, 1971).
Longman III, Tremper, and Peter Enns, eds. *Dictionary of the Old Testament Wisdom, Poetry & Writings* (Downers Grove, IL: InterVarsity, 2008).
Martin, Ralph P., and Peter H. Davids, eds. *Dictionary of the Later New Testament & Its Developments* (Downers Grove, IL: InterVarsity, 1997).

Roberts, Alexander, and James Donaldson, eds. *The Apostolic Fathers*, American Edition.

Schaff, Philip. *History of the Christian Church*, 8 vols. (Grand Rapids: Eerdmans, 1995).

Tenney, Merril C., ed. *The New International Dictionary of the Bible* (Grand Rapids: Zondervan, 1987).

Unger, Merrill F. *Unger's Bible Handbook* (Chicago: Moody Press, 1967).

Walton, John H., and Victor H. Matthews and Mark W. Chavalas. *The IVP Bible Background Commentary: Old Testament* (Downers Grove, IL: InterVarsity, 2000).

Walvoord, John F., and Roy B. Zuck, eds. *The Bible Knowledge Commentary: New Testament* (Wheaton, IL: Victor Books, 1983).

_____. *The Bible Knowledge Commentary: Old Testament* (Wheaton, IL: Victor Books, 1985).

Greek Language Resources

Aland, Kurt, et. al. *The Greek New Testament, Fourth Revised Edition* (Stuttgart: Deutche Bibelgesellschaft/United Bible Societies, 1998).

Balme, Maurice, and Gilbert Lawall. *Athenaze: An Introduction to Ancient Greek*, Book I (New York and Oxford: Oxford University Press, 1990).

Brenton, Sir Lancelot C. L., ed & trans. *The Septuagint With Apocrypha* (Peabody, MA: Hendrickson, 1999).

Bromiley, Geoffrey W., ed. *Theological Dictionary of the New Testament*, abridged (Grand Rapids: Eerdmans, 1985).

Brown, Robert K. and Philip W. Comfort, trans. *The New Greek-English Interlinear New Testament* (Carol Stream, IL: Tyndale House, 1990).

Danker, Frederick William, ed., et. al. *A Greek-English Lexicon of the New Testament and Other Early Christian Literature*, third edition (Chicago: University of Chicago Press, 2000).

Liddell, H.G., and R. Scott. *An Intermediate Greek-English Lexicon* (Oxford: Clarendon Press, 1994).

Metzger, Bruce M. *A Textual Commentary on the Greek New Testament* (London and New York: United Bible Societies, 1975).

Nestle, Erwin, and Kurt Aland, eds. *Novum Testamentum Graece, Nestle-Aland 27th Edition* (Stuttgart: Deutche Bibelgesellschaft, 1993).

Newman, Jr., Barclay M. *A Concise Greek-English Dictionary of the New Testament* (Stuttgart: United Bible Societies/Deutche Bibelgesellschaft, 1971).

Rahlfs, Alfred, ed. *Septuaginta* (Stuttgart: Deutche Bibelgesellschaft, 1979).

Thayer, Joseph H. *Thayer's Greek-English Lexicon of the New Testament* (Peabody, MA: Hendrickson, 2003).

Vine, W.E. *Vine's Expository Dictionary of New Testament Words* (Nashville: Thomas Nelson, 1968).

Zodhiates, Spiros, ed. *Complete Word Study Dictionary: New Testament* (Chattanooga: AMG Publishers, 1993).

Hebrew Language Resources

Arnold, Bill T., and John H. Choi. *A Guide to Biblical Hebrew Syntax* (New York: Cambridge University Press, 2003).

Baker, Warren, and Eugene Carpenter, eds. *Complete Word Study Dictionary: Old Testament* (Chattanooga: AMG Publishers, 2003).

Brown, Francis, S.R. Driver, and Charles A. Briggs. *Hebrew and English Lexicon of the Old Testament* (Oxford: Clarendon Press, 1979).

Davidson, Benjamin. *The Analytical Hebrew and Chaldee Lexicon* (Grand Rapids: Zondervan, 1970).

Dotan, Aron, ed. *Biblia Hebraica Leningradensia* (Peabody, MA: Hendrickson, 2001).

Harris, R. Laird, Gleason L. Archer, Jr., and Bruce K. Waltke, eds. *Theological Wordbook of the Old Testament* (Chicago: Moody Press, 1980).

Holladay, William L., ed. *A Concise Hebrew and Aramaic Lexicon of the Old Testament* (Leiden, the Netherlands: E.J. Brill, 1988).

Jastrow, Marcus. *Dictionary of the Targumim, Talmud Bavli, Talmud Yerushalmi, and Midrashic Literature* (New York: Judaica Treasury, 2004).

Kittel, Rudolph, et. al., eds. *Biblica Hebraica Stuttgartensia* (Stuttgart: Deutche Bibelgesellschaft, 1977).

Koehler, Ludwig, and Walter Baumgartner, eds. *The Hebrew & Aramaic Lexicon of the Old Testament*, 2 vols. (Leiden, the Netherlands: Brill, 2001).

Seow, C.L. *A Grammar for Biblical Hebrew*, revised edition (Nashville: Abingdon, 1995).

תורה נביאים כתובים והברית החדשה (Jerusalem: Bible Society in Israel, 1991).

Unger, Merrill F., and William White. *Nelson's Expository Dictionary of the Old Testament* (Nashville: Thomas Nelson, 1980).

Historical Sources

Bettenson, Henry, and Christ Maunder, eds. *Documents of the Christian Church* (Oxford: Oxford University Press, 1999).

Eusebius: *Ecclesiastical History*, trans. C.F. Cruse (Peabody, MA: Hendrickson, 1998).

Irvin, Dale T., and Scott W. Sunquist. *History of the World Christian Movement*, Vol. 1 (Maryknoll, NY: Orbis Books, 2001).

Josephus, Flavius: *The Works of Josephus: Complete and Unabridged*, trans. William Whiston (Peabody, MA: Hendrickson, 1987).

Judeaus, Philo: *The Works of Philo: Complete and Unabridged*, trans. C.D. Yonge (Peabody, MA: Hendrickson, 1993).

Shanks, Hershel, ed. *Ancient Israel: From Abraham to the Roman Destruction of the Temple* (Washington, D.C.: Biblical Archaeology Society, 1999).

Jewish Reference Sources

Cohen, Abraham. *Everyman's Talmud: The Major Teachings of the Rabbinic Sages* (New York: Schoken, 1995).

Eisenberg, Ronald L. *The JPS Guide to Jewish Traditions* (Philadelphia: Jewish Publication Society, 2004).

Encyclopaedia Judaica. MS Windows 9x. Brooklyn: Judaica Multimedia (Israel) Ltd, 1997.

Hertz, J.H., ed. *Pentateuch & Haftorahs* (London: Soncino, 1960).

Kolatch, Alfred J. *The Jewish Book of Why* (Middle Village, NY: Jonathan David Publishers, 1981).

_____. *The Second Jewish Book of Why* (Middle Village, NY: Jonathan David Publishers, 1985).

Lieber, David L. *Etz Hayim: Torah and Commentary* (New York: Rabbinical Assembly, 2001).

Neusner, Jacob, trans. *The Mishnah: A New Translation* (New Haven and London: Yale University Press, 1988).

_____, and William Scott Green, eds. *Dictionary of Judaism in the Biblical Period* (Peabody, MA: Hendrickson, 2002).

Scherman, Nosson, ed., et. al. *The ArtScroll Chumash, Stone Edition*, 5th ed. (Brooklyn: Mesorah Publications, 2000).

Scherman Nosson, and Meir Zlotowitz, eds. *The Complete ArtScroll Siddur: Nusach Ashkenaz* (Brooklyn: Mesorah Publications, 1984).

Messianic Reference Sources

Cohn-Sherbok, Dan, ed. *Voices of Messianic Judaism* (Baltimore: Lederer Books, 2001).

Stern, David H. *Jewish New Testament Commentary* (Clarksville, MD: Jewish New Testament Publications, 1995).

Software Programs

BibleWorks 5.0. MS Windows 9x. Norfolk: BibleWorks, LLC, 2002. CD-ROM.

BibleWorks 7.0. MS Windows XP. Norfolk: BibleWorks, LLC, 2006. CD-ROM.

BibleWorks 8.0. MS Windows Vista/7 Release. Norfolk: BibleWorks, LLC, 2009-2010. DVD-ROM.

E-Sword 9.9.1. MS Windows Vista/7. Franklin, TN: Equipping Ministries Foundation, 2011.

Judaic Classics Library II. MS Windows 3.1. Brooklyn: Institute for Computers in Jewish Life, 1996. CD-ROM.

Libronix Digital Library System 1.0d: Church History Collection. MS Windows XP. Garland, TX: Galaxie Software. 2002.

TNN Press is the official publishing arm of TNN Online, and its parent organization, Outreach Israel Ministries. TNN Press is dedicated to producing high quality, doctrinally sound, challenging, and fair-minded Messianic materials and resources for the Twenty-First Century. TNN Press offers a wide array of new and exciting books and resources for the truth seeker.

TNN Press titles are available for purchase at

www.outreachisrael.net or at   **amazon.com**

Hebraic Roots: An Introductory Study
is TNN Press' main, best-selling publication, that offers a good overview of the Messianic movement and Messianic lifestyle that can be used for individual or group study in twelve easy lessons

Introduction to Things Messianic
is an excellent companion to *Hebraic Roots*, which goes into substantially more detail into the emerging theology of the Messianic movement, specific areas of Torah observance, and aspects of faith such as salvation and eschatology

The Messianic Helper series, edited by Margaret McKee Huey, includes a series of booklets with instructional information on how to have a Messianic home, including holiday celebration guides. After reading both *Hebraic Roots* and *Introduction to Things Messianic*, these are the publications you need to read!

Messianic Winter Holiday Helper
is a guide to help you during the Winter holiday season, addressing the significance of *Chanukah*, the period of the Maccabees, and the non-Biblical holiday of Christmas

Messianic Spring Holiday Helper
is a guide to assist you during the Spring holiday season, analyzing the importance of *Purim*, Passover and Unleavened Bread, *Shavuot*, and the non-Biblical holiday of Easter

Messianic Fall Holiday Helper
is a guide for the Fall holiday season of *Yom Teruah/Rosh HaShanah, Yom Kippur,* and *Sukkot,* along with reflective teachings and exhortations

Messianic Sabbath Helper (coming soon)
is a guide that will help you make the seventh-day Sabbath a delight, discussing both how to keep the Sabbath and the history of the transition to Sunday that occurred in early Christianity

Messianic Torah Helper (coming soon)
is a guide that will weigh the different perspectives of the Pentateuch present in Jewish and Christian theology, consider the role of the Law for God's people, and how today's Messianics can fairly approach issues of *halachah* and tradition in their Torah observance

Outreach Israel Ministries director **Mark Huey** has written Torah commentaries and reflections that are thought provoking and very enlightening for Messianic Believers today.

TorahScope Volume I
is a compilation workbook of insightful commentaries on the weekly Torah and Haftarah portions

TorahScope Volume II
is a second compilation workbook of expanded commentaries on the weekly Torah and Haftarah portions

TorahScope Volume III
is a third compilation workbook of expanded commentaries on the weekly Torah and Haftarah portions, specifically concentrating on the theme of faith

TorahScope Haftarah Exhortations
is a compilation workbook of insightful commentaries on the specific, weekly Haftarah portions, designed to be used to compliment the weekly Torah reading

TorahScope Apostolic Scripture Reflections
is a compilation workbook of insightful reflections on suggested readings from the Apostolic Scriptures or New Testament, designed to be used to compliment the weekly Torah and Haftarah readings

Counting the Omer: A Daily Devotional Toward Shavuot
is a daily devotional with fifty succinct reflections from Psalms, guiding you during the season between the festivals of Passover and Pentecost

Sayings of the Fathers: A Messianic Perspective on Pirkei Avot
is a daily devotional for two years of reflection on the Mishnah
tractate *Pirkei Avot,* introducing you to some of the key views
present in the Apostolic period as witnessed by the Jewish Sages
(intended to be read during the counting of the *omer*)

TNN Online editor and Messianic apologist **J.K. McKee** has written on
Messianic theology and practice, including studies on Torah observance, the
end-times, and commentaries that are helpful to those who have difficult
questions to answer.

The New Testament Validates Torah
Does the New Testament Really Do Away With the Law?
is a resource examining a wide variety of Biblical passages,
discussing whether or not the Torah of Moses is really abolished
in the New Testament

Torah In the Balance, Volume I
The Validity of the Torah and Its Practical Life Applications
examines the principal areas of a Torah observant walk of faith
for the newcomer, including one's spiritual motives

Confronting Critical Issues (coming soon)
An Analysis of Subjects that Affects the Growth and Stability
of the Emerging Messianic Movement
compiles a variety of articles and analyses that directly confront
negative teachings and trends that have been witnessed in the
broad Messianic community in the past decade

TNN Press has produced a variety of **Messianic commentaries** on
various books of the Bible under the "for the Practical Messianic" byline.
These can be used in an individual, small group, or congregational study.

general commentaries:
A Survey of the Tanach for the Practical Messianic
A Survey of the Apostolic Scriptures for the Practical Messianic

specific book commentaries:
Acts 15 for the Practical Messianic
Galatians for the Practical Messianic
Ephesians for the Practical Messianic
Philippians for the Practical Messianic
Colossians and Philemon for the Practical Messianic
The Pastoral Epistles for the Practical Messianic
1&2 Thessalonians for the Practical Messianic
James for the Practical Messianic (coming soon)
Hebrews for the Practical Messianic

One of the goals of TNN Press is to always be in the mode of producing more cutting edge materials, addressing head on some of the theological and spiritual issues facing our emerging Messianic movement. In addition to our current array of available and soon-to-be available publications, the following are a selection of **Future Projects**, in various stages of planning and pre-production, most of which involve research at the present time (2012). Look for their release sometime over the next two to five years and beyond.

> *Torah In the Balance, Volume II*
> *The Set-Apart Life in Action—The Outward Expressions of*
> *Faith*
> by J.K. McKee
> will examine many of the finer areas of Torah observance, which has a diversity of interpretations and applications as witnessed in both mainstream Judaism and the wide Messianic community

> *Honoring One Another*
> *Mutual Submission and the Future of People in the Broad*
> *Messianic Movement*
> by J.K. McKee
> will consider the sizeable need for today's Messianic community to adopt a mutual submission ideology, where Jewish and non-Jewish Believers can all feel welcome and valued, and husbands and wives can be co-leaders of the home

> *Messianic Kosher Helper*
> will be a guide discussing various aspects of the kosher dietary laws, clean and unclean meats, common Jewish traditions associated with kashrut, and common claims made that these are no longer important for Believers

> *Salvation on the Line*
> by J.K. McKee
> is a planned two-volume work that will directly tackle the subject of apostasy in today's Messianic movement, considering both the Divinity and Messiahship of Yeshua (I) and then the reliability of the Scriptures and human origins (II)